Guarding
the Gospel

Bible, Cross & Mission

Also Available
Fanning the Flame

Guarding the Gospel

Bible, Cross & Mission

Meeting the Challenge in a Changing World

General Editor
Chris Green

GRAND RAPIDS, MICHIGAN 49530 USA

ZONDERVAN.COM/
AUTHOR**TRACKER**

ZONDERVAN™

Guarding the Gospel
Copyright © 2006 by Chris Green

Requests for information should be addressed to:
Zondervan, *Grand Rapids, Michigan 49530*

ISBN-10: 0-310-26741-2
ISBN-13: 978-0-310-26741-6

Chris Green asserts the moral right to be identified as the editor of this work.

Interior design by Tracey Walker

Printed in the United Kingdom

06 07 08 09 10 11 • 10 9 8 7 6 5 4 3 2 1

Contents

Theme 3: Mission

Homosexuality

Conference Addresses

The Way Forward

Contributors

Canon Dr Christina Baxter
Principal of St John's College, Nottingham

Rt Revd Wallace Benn
*Bishop of Lewes, President of the Church of England Evangelical
    Council*

Rt Revd Graham Cray
Bishop of Maidstone

Ven Dr Paul Gardner
*Archdeacon of Exeter, Chairman of the Church of England
    Evangelical Council, and the NEAC 4 Steering Group*

Revd Chris Green
*Vice Principal, Oak Hill Theological College, London, and a
    member of the NEAC 4 Steering Group*

Most Revd and Rt Hon Dr David Hope
Archbishop of York

Professor Edith M. Humphrey
*Associate Professor of New Testament at Pittsburgh Theological
    Seminary*

Most Revd Dr Peter Jensen
Archbishop of Sydney

Rt Revd James Jones
Bishop of Liverpool

Revd Professor Alister McGrath
Principal, Wycliffe Hall, Oxford

Revd Professor David Peterson
Principal, Oak Hill Theological College, London

Revd Vaughan Roberts
Rector, St. Ebbe's Church, Oxford

Contributors

Canon Professor Anthony C. Thiselton
Emeritus Professor in Residence, University of Nottingham

Revd Dr Chris Wright
International Ministry Director of the Langham Partnership International

Professor Gordon J. Wenham
Professor of Old Testament at the University of Gloucester

Most Revd and Rt Hon Dr Rowan Williams
Archbishop of Canterbury

Introduction

The Congress in Context

Chris Green

The papers in this book are only a few of the many that were presented at Blackpool, in the unforgettable mock-baronial setting of the Winter Gardens. There were so many forums and seminars that they simply could not be included. And many of the main stage presentations simply could not be put on to paper. Who could forget Archbishop Josiah Fearon from Nigeria explaining to a packed and silent ballroom that, yes, he expected to die for his faith. Or the explosive passion of Andy Hawthorne putting the challenge of today's youth culture before us. Or Communion to the sound of the Hallelujah Chorus and fireworks.

These papers, then, are the principal addresses on the main stage, on the key Congress themes. They were all given with a view to publication in this form.

It was an extraordinary summer to be meeting, and repeatedly we had to remind one another that the Congress had been three years in the planning, and was not a hasty attempt to grab headlines, or to meet as a 'Council of War' on crises in the Anglican communion.[1] Decisions made in New Westminster, New Hampshire and Oxford, the Primates' meeting in Brazil, and a major international Evangelical Fellowship of the Anglican Communion (EFAC) conference in Nairobi faced us with a sense of purpose and a reason to meet, unexpected and possibly unhelpful in its emphasis, which had perhaps been lacking even six months before.

It certainly helped us focus on the word *Anglican* in a sharper way. Suddenly, people who were in practice hardly allied to a denomination at all discovered that decisions being made in another part of the country, or even the world, were having an impact on their own congregation. I shall never forget being told off by an archdeacon in Kenya for the state of the Church of England, for which I think he held me personally responsible. And to the extent that we might be, we need to face up to our denominational ties and duties. One of the new realities for some at the Congress was that it was precisely because we are evangelical that we are having problems with other parts of the Communion. *Evangelical* and *Anglican* can work together, independently, or in conflict, and the conflict makes one think harder about the contours of loyalty, and the question of which of those two words is the noun and which the adjective. That is work we need to do together, internationally, before the next NEAC.

Which means it is a surprise for many to discover that up to a few months before the Congress, the Steering Group had no intention of mentioning sexuality at all. We had planned that this would be *our* congress on *our* issues, and other questions would for the time being have to be unaddressed. It became clear, though, that although we were trying to avoid the unhealthy interest with labelling us as sex-obsessed bigots, not having an evening on sexuality was going to be eccentric and unhelpful, and so we planned an up-to-date briefing for evangelical Anglicanism. Again, not all of the presentations could be reduced to paper, but the two principal biblical ones are here, and they both break new ground.

Back to Basics?

'Back to Basics' was the title of Prime Minister John Major's ill-fated attempt to reverse the trends that ended his term of office. He tried to capture the essence of political conservatism in the phrase, but it was used against him, trapping him in a lost world of yesteryear.

When NEAC 4 was first suggested around the themes of Bible, Cross and Mission, similar concerns were raised. Surely, said some, a 'Back to Basics' campaign is the last thing we need. And if there had been an attempt to think in that political, or rather *party* political way, those voices were a quite necessary corrective. It is easy, but fatal, to avoid today's hard questions, retreat to the past and fight yesterday's battles with yesterday's slogans.

But there is another sense in which those voices are siren voices. The people of God throughout history have a tendency to forget, and it is a common theme of both Old and New Testament writers that we should 'remember'. It came through in Paul Gardner's Bible readings from 2 Peter, reprinted here. Remembering in this context means a conscious act of the will, to bring into our thoughts and actions the impact of God's work and words. In that sense, 'back to basics' should be the daily cry of every Christian, because we know how easy it is for today's questions to crowd out the Bible, the Cross and our Mission. Rather than drawing the wagons in a circle, as some feared, these three themes expressed a confidence in the finished words and works of God, in the need for us constantly to return to his agenda, rather than ours, and in the unfinished task which lies to hand.[2]

What the steering committee had failed to foresee, although with hindsight it is obvious, is that the Bible, the Cross and Mission are three of the different but connected means which God uses to create unity among his people. As we opened God's word to discover what he says on the three themes, he used his word to create the unity which we had longed for, planned for, worked for and prayed for, which seemed too fragile in prospect but so inevitable and powerful in reality.

That was, in itself, a demonstration of the habit of mind which comes closest to defining evangelicalism: a submissiveness to the whole of the Bible, giving each part its appropriate weight, allowing the defining centre to explain the remainder. Such a pattern frees us from the tyranny of the present, because it is God's word and work which is truly relevant, and frees us from the tyranny of the past, because each generation has to encounter God's word for itself and to encounter those old truths in the face of new and urgent questions.

Defining evangelicals by our intended obedience to God's word is much more useful than defining us by our differences and divisions. No one group or person can claim the unique vantage point from which to survey the terrain, or to occupy the point of balance. After all, isn't it human nature that everyone considers his or her own position to be the most balanced, or the most open to God's Spirit, or to have the clearest perspective on all others? So while the follow-up to NEAC must include addressing crucial theological matters which open up between us, Blackpool focussed on the Bible, which defines us, the Cross, which unites us, and the Mission God has given us, which inspires us. Our identity is found there. The Bible is our boundary, which allows us to debate, and sets the parameters for that debate, the Cross is our centre, uniting us with God and with one another, and Mission is our mandate, as we reach out in God's name to a lost and needy world. Given those, we evangelicals know who we are, and can have a robust discussion on how other issues fit into the frame. We are also much better placed to counter the sloppy clichés of us as mindless happy clappies, thoughtless fundamentalists and ruthless homophobes. These papers should show how out-of-touch such caricatures are.

The old warning is true: what one generation believes, a second assumes, and a third rejects. May we have moved from assuming these things to be true, to knowing them for ourselves, and may we have the courage to contend for them in the hard days ahead.

Notes

1. By BBC Radio 4 in their flagship *Today* programme on the morning of the Congress. It was dropped from later news summaries, perhaps because the journalists found that the programme was not as focussed around sexuality as they might have expected, or wished.
2. For the background to how these three themes were chosen see the preparatory book, *Fanning the Flame*: *Bible, Cross and Mission*, eds. P. Gardner, C. Wright and C. Green (Grand Rapids: Zondervan, 2003).

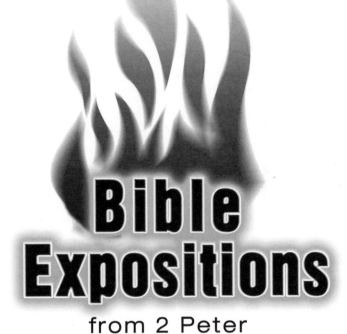

Bible Expositions

from 2 Peter

Bible Expositions from 2 Peter

The Context for Mission:
Three Expositions from 2 Peter

Paul Gardner

The Congress had three Bible expositions at its heart, each taken from 2 Peter, which as Paul Gardner explains, was not what he had initially planned. Quite wonderfully, though, these three passages gave a centrality to the need to be faithful to God and his Gospel, which given the timing and context of the Congress was entirely appropriate.

The Ven Dr Paul Gardner is Archdeacon of Exeter. As the chairman of the Church of England Evangelical Council he chaired the steering group for NEAC 4.

Chapter 1

Participating in the Divine Nature

2 Peter 1:1–10

Sometimes the Holy Spirit impresses himself upon us in interesting ways, and this happened to me with these Bible readings. Given the Congress themes, I was preparing work on 1 John. Yet in early summer as evangelicals united in a remarkable way, I felt God increasingly pointing me to 2 Peter, which is surely a tract for our times. So I pray that God's Spirit will speak to us in his Scripture in a way that will challenge and encourage us all.

Some General Comments

I *do* believe that this epistle was written by the apostle Peter from Rome to a group of churches mostly composed of converted Gentiles, probably in the mid-sixties just before he died a martyr at the hands of Nero. And here, I believe, Peter, knowing he is about to die, as he makes clear in 1:13–14, writes something not unlike a 'last will and testament' in which he stresses all that he believes is vital for these churches.

His main concern for these churches is with false teaching. So he examines these teachings and warns of the danger of judgement. Yet this is by no means a negative book. Peter's counter to false teaching touches on great areas of the glory of the gospel which he begs his readers to recall continuously. He specially highlights four areas of great joy but also of great strategic value when confronted by falsehood. He speaks first of **the joys of our salvation which must lead to a godly and virtuous life**; secondly of **the trustworthiness of Scripture**; thirdly of **the supreme Lordship of Jesus Christ**; and then finally of **Christ's certain return to judge and to save**.

I suppose it ought not to surprise us that all four of these areas are under attack in the church today as well. In an age when our behaviour is defined often in terms of our 'rights' or of what 'feels good', or 'seems natural', then the call for a godly life will be as deeply countercultural for us as it was for the Hellenistic world in which Peter lived. In an age of pluralism, the stress on the supreme Lordship of Jesus Christ is also going to be subject to attack.

As in Peter's day, so in ours, Scripture as God's truthful and utterly trustworthy Word is under attack. Of course, it is just another permutation really of Genesis 3:1 and Satan's question – 'Did God really say?' And that original question of course led to the next serious issue that men and women have sought to avoid or deny right through the ages: will Christ return to judge?

So Peter's epistle, speaking to the attacks on the faith in his day, speaks also to us who face attacks on the faith in all four of these areas. But it begins with Peter reminding his readers of the joys of salvation.

A. The Joys of Salvation – What We Have Received (1:1–4)

1. Christians have received a precious faith – that is, a faith as precious as Peter's and the other apostles (v. 1).

Even though Peter was an apostle and a Jew, these Gentile Christians had *a faith as precious as ours*. 'Faith' here is not the body of doctrine that we might find in a creed, but refers to the believer's own commitment to the Lord Jesus. This commitment to Christ as God and Saviour, is given by God. The word *precious* is a wonderful description.

This faith is a gift that has come through the righteousness of Christ (v. 1). This could refer to God's righteousness, meaning his fairness and justice in giving equal status to all people of faith, whether Jew or Gentile. But here, especially because of the emphasis on 'having *received* it', I think it more likely refers to the righteousness by which God puts people right with himself. We sometimes call this 'imputed' righteousness, a righteousness credited by God to our account so that we may be declared 'not guilty' before his judgement throne.

As Christians face the challenges of false teachers in their midst then the first thing to recall is the joy of salvation. Peter's comments here are more than simply nice opening comments, they are context setting reminders. They are vital reminders that in our context where attacks on the truth, on Christ, on our desire to live holy lives, abound, we still have a most precious faith that is as precious and of the same status as the faith the apostles themselves had obtained.

2. Christians have received a powerful gift

But more than that, among the joys of salvation to be recalled, Peter tells us in verse 3 *that his divine power has given us everything we need for life and godliness through our knowledge of him who called us by his own glory and goodness.* Verses 2 and 3 are closely linked and Peter seems to have directly in mind *Jesus'* divine power by which he has given us all we need for life and godliness. And we have this, says Peter, *through our **knowledge** of him who called us.*

This introduces a theme of knowledge, that runs through the epistle. This knowledge is of course, both the intellectual grasp of who God and Jesus are and what they say and demand, and a personal experience of and commitment to our God and Saviour.

As Richard Bauckham says, this knowledge is 'the fundamental Christian knowledge gained in conversion.'[1] But the sheer joy of what is said here can so easily be missed. Peter will remind us of the call to godliness and our temptation will be to say 'but my desires – even my nature – lead me in another direction'. The joy is that by his grace, he has given us his own divine power to fulfil what he asks of us in every area of life and in our way of living.

Here is at least part of the answer to those even in the church who sit light to the clear ethical and life-style injunctions of Scripture. In my experience many who sit light to issues of justice, or of sexual behaviour, or of greed, or of anger, do so not because they wish to disregard Scripture completely, but rather feel that talking of these things is a 'turnoff' to people. Well, I guess these things often are a 'turnoff' for we are all sinful and selfish. But when we preach the full gospel in all its positive glory and joy that Peter shares with us here, we find that Jesus himself, who himself faced all our temptations, has given us his divine power precisely to cope with the life to which he has called us. Like Peter we should stress the joy of the power rather than the difficulty of the command, and that gospel is truly attractive to people as God draws them to himself.

3. Christians have received very great and precious promises (v. 4)

These are both the promises of God's overflowing grace and protection in the present and also of the eternal kingdom in the future to which verse 11 refers – *there will be richly provided for you an entrance into the eternal kingdom of our Lord and Saviour Jesus Christ.*

Later Peter affirms, against the false teachers, that Jesus will for certain return to judge and to save. So there is great joy in seeing again how much we have received from our Lord.

And what is all this for? Well,

B. The Goal before Us (v. 4b)

So that through them [through receiving the fullness of God's promises] you may become partakers of the divine nature, having escaped from the corruption that is in the world because of sinful desire.

Partakers of the divine nature. What a statement! Peter doesn't mean that we become God. Yet the phrase was probably chosen because it would have rung bells with his readers who had come from a pagan, dualistic background. Peter captures the attention by redefining ideas in the light of God's revelation. There is no sense here of any loss of distinction between the Creator and his creatures as there was in Greek thought, or as there is in New Age thinking today. Yet Peter surely does indeed mean that we are to be, and will, be Godlike, and that we will reflect the person of Jesus in our lives.

Partakers in the divine nature. This will only be completed of course when we have escaped from the corruption of this world, but that it not to say this is simply a promise for the future. Peter is concerned that this staggering participation in the divine nature is to be seen in our lives today. We *already* share, by grace, in some of God's attributes. For instance, Christians are called to be 'holy'. Holiness is a characteristic of the divine nature. Yes, one day we will be perfected, but growth in holiness is already to be visible in the life of the person who comes to the knowledge of the Lord. And Christians also share in God's immortality. We are not trapped in this world. We will inherit the eternal kingdom (v. 11).

The appeal Peter makes, then, as he calls us to reflect on the joy of our salvation, is that we become and are to become partakers in the divine nature. So, *For this very reason,* says Peter (v. 5), there should be a proper Christian response even now, which is where he turns.

C. The Christian Response (1:5 – 10)

With Christ's divine power, we cannot give up in despair. We can't say 'Christian holiness is possible for some but not for me'. God has given us the power to lead an effective and productive life and so not be *ineffective or unfruitful* (v. 8).

The list of virtues Peter gives here are not, I think, in any special order, except to say that the knowledge of God starts with faith and ends with the mark of the Christian: love. And we are to chase after these with eagerness and effort (v. 10) for they become evidence to us and to others that our call and election is sure, and they constantly remind us of the great day when we will be welcomed into the eternal kingdom.

Peter is setting up a distinction he will develop in chapter two. The faithful will seek after God and will wish to respond in every area of their life to his grace and calling, but those who follow false teaching will end up with no such desire and make no such effort.

Peter's emphasis here in this list is one which we as evangelicals need to look at again in our age. How do we present ourselves to our world? As we talk of Christ, does the world see in us a people who share in that divine nature? What do they see of divine 'goodness' among us? It is disturbing but perhaps not unsurprising that people these days even in the church tend to assume that goodness really simply means being 'nice people'.

For some, being loving is indistinguishable from being thought to be 'nice' by all. Yet, some of these attributes here are so counter-cultural in our age, just as in Peter's time, that there's no way people exercising them will always be seen as 'nice'. A call to 'self control', for example, will never go down well in this day and age, but it will reflect the divine nature. We only have to see how defensive some of our newspapers were this summer about the loutish behaviour of drunken English tourists to know that 'self control' is not a virtue our nation cherishes. And what about 'goodness'? I am sure I am not alone in having seen people come to faith only to find they have within a few months, lost their job as they have refused to lie or cheat or steal. They may not be popular, but their counter-cultural stand reflects God's goodness.

Perseverance is about a total and practical commitment to the sovereign Lord and Saviour even when we are suffering. This also speaks against the flow of our culture where the emphasis on pragmatism means that if something causes suffering, or isn't working or giving us good feelings we should change and move our position. But no matter how countercultural will be the life we live, it is the remembrance of sin forgiven that will always form the background to our thinking.

Peter doesn't beat around the bush. If we don't respond with a reflection of the divine nature in this way then it is as if we were blind, but most importantly, it reflects the fact that we have forgotten Christ's saving work of forgiveness (v. 9). We have forgotten the cross and the cleansing of past sins. We have forgotten all that Peter has been rejoicing in earlier in the passage.

Peter's challenge, then, cannot and must not be missed for us in this day and age. One of our problems, I believe, is our tendency to be a people who are often indistinguishable from the world. We've become a people who have forgotten the cross, and the mercies of Christ, and the joys of our salvation, and therefore become a people who have often been unfaithful to the call to reflect the divine nature. Where once a legalistic pietism may have been an evangelical problem, now we easily ignore the call to a whole life response to God's salvation that reflects the divine nature.

So, this passage causes us to rejoice as we remember all that we have received in Christ, even to the extent that we participate in the divine nature. Our response, through the divine power we have been given, is to reflect that nature even now. And then one day we will receive a rich welcome into the eternal kingdom of our Lord and Saviour Jesus Christ.

Notes

1. Bauckham, R.J. *Jude, 2 Peter* (Waco, TX: Word, 1983) p. 178.

Chapter 2

Encountering False Teaching

2 Peter 1:12-21

In the last section we saw how Peter stressed the joy of what we have received by grace through our Lord Jesus Christ: the divine power he has given us, the great and precious promises that we have through his glory and goodness, and the staggering privilege of partaking in the divine nature. We heard his challenge to live now as reflecting that nature, and never to forget the forgiveness of sins. Christ is at the heart of it all.

Now, Peter moves from this great positive gospel statement and appeal, into handling the attacks of false teachers.

A. The Urgent Reminder (1:12–15)

So important is what Peter says that he insists his readers are to *remember* the matters of which he has been speaking *always*, even if they know them well! Look at the repetition in 1:12–15:

> *So I will always **remind you of these things,** even though you know them and are firmly established in the truth you now have. I think it is right to **refresh your memory** as long as I live in the tent of this body, because I know that I will soon put it aside, as our Lord Jesus Christ has made clear to me. And I will make every effort to see that after my departure you will always be able to **remember these things**.*

Or in chapter three verses 2, 5 and 8:

> *I want you to recall the words spoken in the past by the holy prophets and the command given by our Lord and Saviour through your apostles ... But they deliberately forget that long ago by God's word the heavens existed and the earth was formed out of water and by water ... But do not forget this one thing, dear friends: With the Lord a day is like a thousand years, and a thousand years are like a day.*

It's there in 3:1 after the examples of false teachers in chapter 2. It's there in 3:2. It's contrasted with the forgetfulness of the false teachers in 3:5. It's there in 3:8. Remember these things.

Perhaps we feel we are firmly established in the truth (as 1:12 puts it) and as good evangelicals we don't need to spend time on these things! Peter's concern is that complacency lays us all open to false teaching.

We *will* encounter false teaching (2:1)

The fact is that we will all encounter false teaching ... *just as there will be false teachers among you, who will secretly bring in destructive heresies.* Note, it will happen *secretly.* As we have found in recent years in a number of areas, false teaching is suddenly upon us. Jesus himself warned of the same danger in Matthew 7, *Watch out for false prophets. They come to you in sheep's clothing.*

In 3:3 Peter is keen for us to see that the presence of scoffers and false teaching is actually a mark of the last days, the days in which we live. Peter follows the prophets and the apostles who were worried about false teachers primarily because they are or will be among us.

So, as Peter bridges into a detailed account of false teaching in chapter 2, he is concerned both that we remember the full gospel for our own joy, and trust the great promises. In that way we can live as God wants. We remember for joy and for life, but also so we can withstand false teaching. As we are told that we shouldn't believe something or trust some Scripture, we remember what is true and what we have received. And we remember in order to withstand false teaching. Sometimes particular truth claims will be attacked. At other times the challenge will be more general. Here the strongest attack is reserved for the glorious second coming of Christ who returns to judge and to save.

B. The Presenting Issue – Is Christ's Return as Judge a Myth? (v. 16)

It seems some people have said Christ's return is a myth. Perhaps they argued that the apostles had invented the story to put fear into people as a means of moral control. It sounds quite modern, doesn't it?

But this passage helps us see how Peter deals with such false teaching. Behind this specific problem, Peter sees a challenge to the truth of Revelation itself. And when he looks at the attack on the trustworthiness of the Scriptures, he points out that it is also an attack on the sovereignty of Christ himself. Chapter 2:1 makes that point explicit. An attack on Christ's return (which is one example of false teaching) leads to a denial of trustworthiness of Scripture, which in turn leads to a denial of Lordship of Christ.

I'll develop that in the third Bible reading. For now, we need to learn from Peter that we will encounter false teaching and, if we are ever to combat falsehood, we must recognise what lies behind the challenges of false teachers. The issue is whether the apostles and Scripture are accepted as trustworthy or not.

C. Peter Defends the Truth of What the Apostles Have Taught (1:17 – 21)

1. The trustworthiness of what was seen and heard by the apostles (vv. 16 – 18)

So Peter turns us first to the trustworthiness of what was seen and heard by the apostles – and he specifically appeals to the transfiguration. There he says, *we*, (Peter James and John, as we know from Matthew 17) were eyewitnesses of Christ in his messianic and judging glory. At the transfiguration they saw a divinely given preview of Christ, the glorified King. Theirs is the eyewitness testimony to this event. But the event itself needed interpretation, and so Peter depends not just on what they *saw* but also on what they *heard*: *This is my Son, whom I love; with him I am well pleased.*

Those are virtually the same words as in Matthew. Here the Father brings together two Old Testament texts. The first part draws on Psalm 2, a psalm full of Messianic expectation, which speaks of the Son who will rule the nations. The second part draws on Isaiah 42:1 which speaks of the suffering servant but also of that servant's role in bringing just judgement to the nations

> *Here is my servant, whom I uphold, my chosen one in whom I delight; I will put my Spirit on him and he will bring justice to the nations. (Isaiah 42:1)*

The apostles *were eyewitnesses* of Christ in his kingly glory (v. 16), and they had heard that verdict pronounced by the Father (v. 18). But how interesting it is that Peter turns to the transfiguration to defend Christ's return to judge. You see, in order to do this he depends on understanding the Father's words of explanation in their Old Testament context, which is a context of messianic coming and judgement. Even the high mountain on which the transfiguration took place helps provide a context for the quotation from Psalm 2:6–7, where we read:

> *'I have installed my King*
> *   on Zion, my holy hill.'*
> *I will proclaim the decree of the LORD:*
> *He said to me, 'You are my Son;*
> *   today I have become your Father'.*

The coming is also guaranteed with the future tense of Psalm 2:9, and the use of that coming as a warning of judgement to come is established in Psalm 2:10

> *'You will rule them with an iron sceptre;*
> *   you will dash them to pieces like pottery.'*
> *Therefore, you kings, be wise; be warned, you rulers of the earth.*

So Peter says this teaching about Christ's return is trustworthy because of apostolic eyewitness and God's word of explanation which has been given context by the Scripture from which it is taken. The transfiguration was a divinely given preview of the second coming.

2. The trustworthiness of Scripture (v. 19)

Second, Peter turns to the trustworthiness of Scripture. While Peter may have had some particular promises from the Old Testament prophets in mind that refer to the second coming, it is more likely that, like Jesus himself on the road to Emmaus, Peter sees the whole of the Old Testament as trustworthy revelation about Christ himself and about his coming in glory as king and judge and Saviour.

He makes the point that *until the Day dawns* this prophetic witness is glorious evidence of the truth of what he says. Scripture is the star that shines in our world now, the dark place, until the full glory is revealed at the Lord's coming.

Until Jesus once again returns personally the prophetic lamp and the apostolic lamp (Scriptures) shine out for us with the light of Christ, a light that remains until the day dawns and the morning star rises. The idea of the morning star is drawn from Numbers 24:17 and various other places in the Old Testament and is a messianic text referring to the coming of the great ruler for Israel.

So the light that we have now, Peter is saying, is Scripture. And he says *you will do well to pay attention to it*. Why? Well, because here it is that, under the Spirit's inspiration, we learn of the things of which he is talking – the great and precious promises; the redemptive work of Christ; the forgiveness of sin; the power that we have been given to live godly lives; what godly lives are to look like, and, specially here, the coming in glory. But here we also learn what is false about false teaching.

But then this leads to questions of why these documents should be trusted, and so Peter turns to,

3. The divine origin of Scripture (vv. 20–21)

Scripture carries God's own authority (v. 21), for as the prophets spoke they did so from God. This cuts right to the heart of some of the issues surrounding our modern debates over the extent of Scriptural inspiration.

Peter is arguing in verse 20, that it is not just the prophecy that is from God but the interpretation that the prophets give to their dreams, visions, etc that is given by God and fully trustworthy.

We must understand this *first of all*, Peter says. It is a critical point.

The false teachers as we see in chapter 2 were rejecting the authority of the prophets, specifically as God's Word. They were giving their own interpretations. They were denying those bits that did not suit their wisdom or the culture of their day, or that undermined their own supposed authority. And just as it was then, so it is today. Often Scripture is the peg on which we hang our own ideas. Peter is saying, it isn't just the dream or the vision, or the story, or the law that comes from God, but the interpretation itself comes from God as these men were carried along by the Spirit. This doesn't mean we avoid the work of studying to make sure we have understood the biblical writers, but it does mean that we trust and follow what we find there.

For those who are finding this rather tough going, let me give a different example from the second coming, but one we often encounter. Many false teachers today will appeal to the law to 'love your neighbour as yourself'. But they give this law their own interpretation, denying the inspired interpretation of that law within Scripture itself. So for example, they would rather not link with their understanding of love any idea of obedience, even though Scriptures tell us that loving your neighbour sums up ideas like 'not coveting', 'not stealing', not committing adultery', and so on. This is the problem we face again and again with false teaching. It often affirms something of God's Word but denies the Spirit-inspired explanation and interpretation of that word which is often deeply countercultural.

So Peter insists on the divine origin and inspiration of Old Testament Scripture both in its account of events and dreams and visions, but also in its interpretation of those events.

How important it is for us today to hear this as we think of the nature of the revelation in Scripture. The spoken words had been the key to understanding what had been seen by Peter at the transfiguration. Fascinatingly, even those words were from Scripture. For Peter to understand the transfiguration as a preview and guarantee of the second coming, he had to know the context in Scripture of the words used by the Father, and he had to trust the prophet and psalmist and their interpretation and explanation in the same way that he had trusted what he had heard directly from the Father. So he allows the messianic context of Psalm 2 and the ruling, judging servant context of Isaiah 41 to help him understand the Father's words and what he has seen and to put it all together.

Incidentally, I think this helps us understand the rather difficult first words of verse 19, *And we have the prophetic word made more sure*. The question in a nutshell is 'does this imply that Peter regarded the Old Testament as "more certain" than apostolic eyewitness?' I doubt that!

It is at least possible that what Peter is saying is that, though what the apostles saw and heard provides fully trustworthy evidence, even what they saw and heard actually needed the Old Testament for its full or 'sure' explanation, for the prophetic word is also God's word on the matter.

What I am saying is that, simply on their own, the Father's words do not clearly demonstrate that Jesus will return to judge. However, once those words are seen in their Old Testament context where there is a fully inspired God-given interpretation and explanation of the role of the Son and the servant, both what the apostles saw and heard become firm evidence for Christ's second coming. The interpretation is, as Peter has shown, inspired of God.

Peter's final point at the end of verse 21 returns to the *how* of inspiration. It happens through the dynamic work of the Holy Spirit in carrying along the prophets, and so he explains how what they say is actually what God says, *From God*.

Application is almost self-evident. The passage shows us that the context for mission in the last days will be one where we do encounter false teaching and it should not surprise us. As we encounter false teaching, Peter has shown us that at its heart will be a challenge to the veracity of Scripture, not the apostolic and prophetic witness.

There will then have to be a response that does two things: first, it must deal with the presenting issue of the false teaching, and secondly, it must go back further into the nature of divine revelation in Scripture. Of course, often it will be our defence of biblical truth on the presenting issue that is picked up and makes the headlines.

Had there been news media in Peter's world they might legitimately have asked whether Peter was 'obsessed' with the second coming, much as we are sometimes accused of being obsessed with sex. The answer is actually 'no'. Peter was not obsessed with that, and nor are we – but people will not always see or hear that. What we are obsessed with is our Lord and Saviour Jesus Christ, who has so graciously spoken to us in Scripture and who has come among us in Christ, who forgives us and loves us and wants all people to come to repentance as Peter puts it in 3:9. But when we so love this Lord then at different times in history the attacks will come in different places and we must answer from God's Word the presenting issue and show why it is important, and what God has to say on the matter. But we must also do what Peter does and really come back to something even more vital, to the utter trustworthiness of Scripture which is almost always what is really under attack.

Living in the Light of Christ's Return

2 Peter 3:1–18

O ver the previous two Bible readings we have seen something of the context for mission as the apostle Peter saw it. The glorious gospel he spelled out so succinctly in the first eleven verses must always be remembered for it energises our ministries and keeps us from being ineffectual or unfruitful, and helps us ward off false teaching.

But the context for our mission also means encountering false teachers. They will attack certain specific teachings, but we must also see how behind those attacks lies a distrust of the truth of Scripture and even a denial of the sovereign lordship of Christ. So let me pick up that point as I said I would.

The False Teachers Deny Jesus As Lord

Peter makes the point clearly in 2:1. These people *will secretly bring in destructive heresies, even denying the Master who bought them* (2:1, ESV). The sovereign lordship of Christ is a key doctrine for Peter which comes through in a number of ways here. He talks of the false teachers denying the Master. But this is not just any master, it is the one who died for them, who *bought them*. This is the crucified Lord they deny, and yet his lordship ironically is going to be seen in the *swift destruction* they bring on themselves.

The use of this word *master* here (in Greek, *despotēs*) suggests lordship with the special sense of one who commands. And as we shall see in chapter 3, one of the things that differentiates Christians and others is how they regard the commandments of the Lord and Saviour (3:2). This word for *master* is a word only used four other times in Scripture of Christ and always refers to his commanding authority. Their denial of Christ's lordship here has in mind their behaviour which Peter goes on to describe in chapter 2, but it also describes their teachings, for they secretly introduce *destructive heresies.*

That this denial of lordship is serious comes through here and in chapter 3 where they *deliberately forget* (v. 5) the power of God's creative and judging word.

The opposite of this denial is spelled out through the epistle by Peter with his lovely full description for Christ which is not used anywhere else in the New Testament. He speaks of *Our Lord and Saviour Jesus Christ.* It's there in 1:11, 2:20 and 3:18. He also uses *God and Saviour Jesus Christ* in 1:1 and twice he uses the more common New Testament title of Lord Jesus Christ.

For Peter, Jesus is the Sovereign King and Judge and Saviour, the glorified King he had seen in the transfiguration, and that is why he is to be worshipped and obeyed and why his word can be trusted.

The denial of the prophetic word, their deliberate overlooking of God's power, and their refusal to acknowledge the return in power and glory of Christ as Scripture and the apostles have taught, leads inevitably to a denial of Christ as Master and Lord.

So let's turn to chapter 3.

A. A Legitimate Question – 'When Is He Coming?' (3:4)

Over the years I have often heard people who are either new to the Christian faith or just interested to find out more ask the question, *Where is the promise of his coming? For ever since the fathers fell asleep, all things are continuing as they were from the beginning of creation.* (3:4, ESV)

Of course, in this context, it is not a genuine question but one that comes from the false teachers and 'scoffers' as they're called in verse 3. Peter brings us back to the issue he addressed in chapter 1. And as he writes to encourage and stir up the sincere mind of these beloved believers (v. 1) he asks us to consider three things.

B. Peter Stirs Up the Believers (3:1 – 10)

First, Peter stirs up the believers to consider four truths.

1. Consider the words of Scripture and of Christ (vv. 1 – 2)

Peter talks of this letter and a previous one, perhaps what we know of as 1 Peter, though not necessarily so, and he again says that he has written these to *remind* them in order *to stimulate them to sincere or wholesome thinking.* Peter wants these Christians to develop what the American side of my family would call a 'mind-set' – a whole way of thinking and living. The Christian faith is not just an assent to a body of doctrine, nor is it just about nice feelings of a new relationship with Jesus. It is so much more than that. It involves developing a godly framework of thinking and living and this, he tells us in verse 2, is built on recalling, going over, remembering Scripture, the predictions of the prophets, and the command of Jesus himself. The *command* of Jesus that Peter refers to is concerned with Jesus' teaching, and command, specially concerning our ethics and behaviour in the last days.

The heretics may *scoff,* and he comes back to that in verses 3 – 4, but our duty first and foremost is to develop a mind-set not formed out of cynicism or doubt, not pulled away from the truth by such false teachers but guided and governed by Scripture and by Christ himself whose word comes to us *through your apostles.* What the apostles have passed on is the word of Christ.

From Scripture, Peter stirs up his readers by calling on them to consider God.

2. Consider that God is Creator and judge (vv. 5–7)

While false teachers deliberately forget that God is the one who created the heavens and the earth and he is the one who has made this promise of Christ's coming, Christians should remember that God is the one who judged the earth with the flood in the days of Noah.

Peter's point here is simple but profound: just remember who made the promise! The one who by his Word created the world from the parting of waters (Genesis 1:6) is the God who at his Word judged the world by water in the days of Noah. He is the Creator and has already shown he is judge. Then,

3. Consider that God is not like us! (v. 8)

> But do not forget this one thing, dear friends: With the Lord a day is like a thousand years, and a thousand years are like a day. The Lord is not slow in keeping his promise, as some understand slowness. (2 Peter 3:8)

God does not figure time in the way we do. That is not to say there is no present or future for God. It's not to say that somehow time doesn't exist for God, for he created it after all. But it is to say that our tiny minds are unlikely to count time as long or short in the way God does.

God will keep his promises at some date into the future. So Peter insists that we shouldn't worry about the delay in spite of the ridicule of false teachers, because this great creator God who himself created time is the one who has made the promise that Christ will return, and return he will.

4. Consider that God is patient (v. 9)

Why does God delay in sending his Son a second time to judge and to save? While a cynical question on the lips of false teachers, it is a genuine question on the lips of believers. Peter's answer gives us a key to the whole Bible and to God's dealings with human beings down over the centuries. Look at the whole of verse 9:

The Lord is not slow in keeping his promise, as some understand slowness. He is patient with you, not wanting anyone to perish, but everyone to come to repentance.

Here is the wonderful and loving God Christians believe in and the one we have preached about for centuries. And surely this is the God we want our church and our nation to hear about. Here we see the mission heart of God. He is a loving God who has not sent Jesus yet to bring an end to this world order, because he is patient with us, not wanting anyone to perish, but rather wanting everyone to come to repentance.

Here is the love of the Lord expressed so clearly to us. Yes, Jesus will return and he will return at some time in the future to save and to judge, and Peter doesn't want us to lose sight of that. *The day of the Lord will come like a thief. The heavens will disappear with a roar; the elements will be destroyed by fire, and the earth and everything in it will be laid bare* (v. 10). There won't be any escaping that day. It will come. But what Peter wants us to know today is that the Lord in his love is being patient. He is giving time for repentance. This is the gospel. There is time and opportunity to repent of sin, to turn to Christ and to receive forgiveness and mercy from the God of all creation, the one who always keeps his word.

C. A Christian Mind-Set (3:11 – 18)

Peter has argued for the truth of the teaching that Christ will return and shown how it must drive our thinking. Hence in verse 11 he asks, *What kind of people ought you to be?* His answer is given by way of three commands. The first is indicated in verse 11.

1. Live holy and godly lives in joyful anticipation of the coming

There is no fear for Christians who await the Lord's return (v. 12). We look forward to it and pray for it and anticipate the glorious day. But more than that. As we live these godly lives so we play a part in hastening the coming of that day.

Conversion and the creation of a holy people for himself and to his glory is God's purpose while this earth lasts. As we join that people, so in a remarkable way we are being told that Christ's coming approaches.

In Acts 3:19–20 Peter said something similar: *Repent, then, and turn to God, so that your sins may be wiped out, so that times of refreshing may come from the Lord, and so that he may send the Christ, who has been appointed for you – even Jesus.*

Peter is saying that if we want Christ to return then we need to be the holy and godly people that he has called us to be. We have already seen that a danger in our modern church is that we rarely talk of holiness or godliness and are often indistinguishable from everyone else. Another danger is that we are so preoccupied with our life and world that the second coming has become a dry doctrine to be remembered at Advent, rather than a rousing and stirring-up reminder of God's missionary heart that we should share.

Rather than being products of a counterculture, a biblical/Jesus culture, rather than being seen to have a radically different mind-set, rather than hastening the day of the Lord, we often seem more to be products of the culture around us. Peter makes the same point again in verse 14. *So then, beloved, since you are looking forward to this, make every effort to be found spotless, blameless and at peace with him.* And his summary is there in verse 15 – what tremendous words – *bear in mind that our Lord's patience means salvation.*

We must pass over Peter's comment on Paul's writing, except to note that already some of Paul's letters were being treated as Scripture and thus fully the trustworthy Word of God

But Peter then returns to his main subject. What kind of people?

2. Hold fast to the truth, and be on your guard

Therefore, beloved, since you already know this, be on your guard so that you may not be carried away by the error of lawless people and fall from your secure position. (v. 17)

When Peter mentions here the 'error of lawless people', he is thinking again of those who have not remembered or followed the commandment of the Lord, people who have been disobedient to Christ.

Yet again then as Peter draws to a close he asks us to remember that any one of us can be led astray. Being on your guard means constantly remembering these things as Peter puts it.

And finally Peter draws it all together in verse 18. What kind of people? People who ...

3. Grow in the grace and knowledge of our Lord and Saviour Jesus Christ.

In the Christian faith we come to know God in the first place by grace. But all subsequent growth in the Christian life is also by grace, by God's continuing gracious work in our lives through the power of his Spirit. He has given us *his divine power.* Growing as Christians and maturing in the faith is about finding God at work within us and following him and remembering the gospel day by day in such a way that we begin to conform more and more to the likeness of Jesus himself.

Growth in *knowledge* of our Lord and Saviour Jesus Christ looks to our coming to an ever deepening relationship with Christ and ever deeper appreciation of who he is and what he has done for us and how wonderful are his promises. Herein lies our Christian joy, but here also lies our defence against the false teachers.

I wonder as we go away from this Congress whether we shall go away with a renewed intention to look at ourselves and guard ourselves in the face of false teaching. Will we simply go away with the same views we came with, or will we go away encouraged by Peter and by each other to look again at the context of our mission and so rejoice more fully and more openly and more evangelistically in the gospel that is ours? And will we go away determined to keep guarding ourselves and examining ourselves to see that we hold still more strongly than before to the utter trustworthiness of Scripture as the Word of God. Will we ask ourselves again whether we trust fully in the total sovereign power of our Lord and Saviour Jesus Christ?

May we all grow in the grace and knowledge of our Lord and Saviour, to whom be the glory both now and to that wonderful day of eternity.

The Bible

Theme 1

Theme 1: The Bible

Graham Cray, David Peterson, and Christina Baxter

Graham Cray and David Peterson worked together closely on their two papers, and they were actually presented at the Congress as four interwoven talks. There had been a genuine meeting of minds between these two men, and that can be seen as they approach the vital question of biblical authority from two opposite, but necessary, directions. Christina Baxter's paper was presented extempore, with passion.

The Rt Revd Graham Cray is Bishop of Maidstone

The Revd Professor David Peterson is the Principal of Oak Hill Theological College, London

Canon Dr Christina Baxter is the Principal of St John's College, Nottingham

Chapter 4

Scriptural Truth in a Postmodern Age

Graham Cray

Introduction

This chapter, together with the one by David Peterson, is about the truth and sufficiency of Scripture, both as the ultimate authority under God for all Christians at all times, but also with particular reference to the postmodern age in which we live. I focus primarily on the theme of scriptural truth and David on scriptural sufficiency. However, our shared intention is to contribute to a Church of England which not only believes Scripture, but which also obeys it!

A. Scriptural Truth on the Front Line

The Bible has a place of unique authority in the Church of God. John Stott explains this with typical clarity. 'The Bible is a unique book: no other book resembles it. For it is God's Word through human words.'[1] But if the Bible is God's Word, from one point of view, who am I to defend it? Spurgeon's great saying is well known, but still worth repeating. 'Defend the Bible? I would just as soon defend a lion. Just turn the Bible loose. It will defend itself.'

However, if Scripture itself calls us always to be ready to give an account for the hope we have in God's Son, his Incarnate Word

(1 Peter 3:15), then it is also reasonable that we be prepared to give an account for our trust in God's written Word.

At this point I want to make a vital distinction between our defense of Scripture – which is always in response to the challenges made, and questions asked, by the society of our time, and so always takes place on today's cultural front line – and the central theological reasons why we recognize and submit to God's authority through Scripture, which hold true, irrespective of our particular cultural context.

For the remainder of this section I will focus on our response to contemporary challenges about Scripture and truth. So to the front line we must go.

But the first thing we find is that during the lifetime of most of the people attending NEAC4 the frontline has moved.

The old front line

The evangelical movement, as we know it, took its shape in relation to the Enlightenment. It was forged in the fires of the evangelical revival to establish a form of biblically faithful Christianity at a time of cultural change. As David Bebbington pointed out in his history, it had clear continuity with previous forms of Scripture-centred Christianity, but also had some new emphases.[2] In other words it was a good piece of gospel and culture work.

On that front line the enemy was Enlightenment rationalism, and increasingly skepticism and secularism, which challenged:

The historical trustworthiness of Scripture
The credibility of a supernatural worldview
The supreme authority of Scripture

These have been the front-line issues for evangelical apologetics. And in their defense some key concepts were marshaled:

The Inspiration of Scripture by the Holy Spirit
The Sufficiency of Scripture; that no other authority is equal

British evangelicals emphasized the *Infallibility* of Scripture, by which they meant it could not fail in the great purposes for which it was given. In the United States, by contrast, *Inerrancy* became a key term.

All of these emphases and expressions had an important history in previous eras of the church, but they became our key concepts in the new battle. At times in our history we have been to battle with one another over these terms.

What we now need most is a united stance on Scripture, because there is still vital action to be taken on the old frontier. Christianity is a history-based faith, or it is groundless. If the great saving events of Scripture did not happen – we have believed in vain. Above all this applies to the resurrection of Christ, as St. Paul makes crystal clear in 1 Corinthians 15:

> *But if it is preached that Christ has been raised from the dead, how can some of you say that there is no resurrection of the dead? If there is no resurrection of the dead, then not even Christ has been raised. And if Christ has not been raised, our preaching is useless and so is your faith. More than that, we are then found to be false witnesses about God, for we have testified about God that he raised Christ from the dead. But he did not raise him if in fact the dead are not raised. For if the dead are not raised, then Christ has not been raised either. And if Christ has not been raised, your faith is futile; you are still in your sins. Then those also who have fallen asleep in Christ are lost. If only for this life we have hope in Christ, we are to be pitied more than all men.*[3]

Reverent biblical and historical scholarship remains essential to our cause. We need to thank God for the reverent scholarship carried out at places like Tyndale House in Cambridge and give it our full support. We have nothing to fear from godly scholarship!

The essential basis of evangelical unity on the old frontier must be this: The complete truthfulness, trustworthiness and sufficiency of Scripture for everything for which it was given, by the inspiration of the Holy Spirit. At the centre of which is salvation through Jesus Christ.

We may debate the precise boundaries of this statement, but at its heart we need to stand united.

The Battle Has Moved On

However, the cultural battle lines have also moved on. To illustrate from the Second World War: 'Remember the Maginot Line'. Determined to learn from their First World War experience, the French created a huge defensive line. Defensive forces were massed to hold it. But the enemy came another way, and outflanked it completely. In the same way the battle for scriptural truth is now on ...

The new front line

What we now face is not so much a direct assault on the truth of the Bible, but a direct assault on the received concept of truth itself. 'The twentieth century has seen the collapse of the traditional concept of truth.'[4] If the old frontier was in the context of the emergence of modernity, the new is shaped by the emergence of postmodernity.

The key issues of the Postmodern Challenge are these:

- Language is seen as indeterminate (so all really is interpretation)
- Truth is a cultural construct. It is not discovered, it is constructed
- Truth is fluid what we are believing for now (at best)
- Truth claims are power plays, a form of oppression at worst.
- And, if this is the nature of language and of truth, then
- Relativism is self-evident

We need to address these in turn.

Language is indeterminate?

Hear the American philosopher Richard Rorty. 'We need to make a distinction between the claim that the world is out there and the claim that truth is out there. To say that the world is out there, that it is not our creation, is to say, with common sense, that most things in space and time are the effects of causes which do not include human mental states. To say that truth is not out there is simply to say that where there are no sentences there is no truth, that sentences are elements of human languages, and that human languages are human creations. The suggestion that truth, as well as the world, is out there is a legacy of an age in which the world was seen as the creation of a being who had a language of his own.'[5]

There lies the clue. 'The world was seen as the creation of a being who had a language of his own.' Christians still see the world that way. Language has meaning because we are created by a communicating God.

The philosopher Nietzsche is the intellectual godfather of this whole contemporary way of thinking. He once wrote, 'I fear we shall never be rid of God, so long as we still believe in grammar.'[6] To which more recently the Jewish philosopher George Steiner replied 'Grammar lives because there is the wager on God.'[7]

Human language has meaning because the Creator exists and communicates. If we believe that, we cannot claim that . . .

Everything is interpretation

If there were no God, or if God did not communicate, we might agree with Jacques Derrida that 'There is nothing outside the text.'[8] But the existence of a God who gives his human creatures the gift of meaningful language sets limits to the possible range of interpretation – whether of Scripture or any other text.

Truth a construct?

So is truth a construct rather than a discovery? To an extent, yes. The search for meaning lies at the heart of what it means to be human. Fallen humans, made in God's image, have always sought the meaning of their lives and constructed the best philosophies or theologies they could.

But now we live in a day which has lost its belief in revealed truth or even in objective truth. This reduces us to truth creation by pick and mix. As the singer Richard Ashcroft said, 'I think there are millions of us on this planet, going through life with no fixed religion, no fixed philosophy, but gathering bits of books, bits of other people's discoveries over the centuries and putting them together with their own lives and forming a new religion, a new philosophy. It isn't a religious thing or a God thing – it's a personal thing, a personal quest to find enlightenment in me.'[9]

Fluid truth?

That sort of truth IS fluid. It is truth for now, truth while it suits me. Surfing on the current fashions of truth until a more attractive wave overtakes me.

You will have noticed the subtle transition from quoting philosophers to quoting pop stars. Many ordinary people share these views, simply because they seem to be real to life, to be common sense. Philosophy and popular culture combine to make postmodernism seem obvious: Especially to those who have never heard of postmodernism!

Relativism seems obvious

If you are continually bombarded with conflicting messages, how can you decide which seem true? In an age of communication overload, objective truth quickly becomes a casualty. 'It once seemed easy enough to distinguish between truth and falsity, objectivity and subjectivity, good reasons and bad, and even morality and immorality. Yet, those days have largely vanished, as television, radio, books, newspapers, e-mail and passing acquaintances inundate us with differences in perspective, values, and understandings. In what particular words can we place our trust when confronted with infinite variations in the real and the good?'[10] In such a world 'The truth' becomes 'my truth' or 'your truth'.

People are rarely relativists in practice, but they find it increasingly hard to justify truth claims as more than personal choices, or something that allegedly 'everybody knows'. In fact it is those who are most sure that their truth is 'The Truth' who are the objects of the greatest suspicion. Because truth claims are increasingly seen as power-plays.

Truth claims as power plays?

'All thought that pretends to discover truth is but an expression of the will to power – even to domination – of those making the truth claims over those who are being addressed by them.'[11]

The statement 'I believe this is true' is interpreted as 'I want power over you by getting you to accept my truth as The Truth.' We must resist the attempt to restrict all language about truth to the category of power. 'Christian theology cannot be compatible with a transvaluation of questions about truth into questions about value or power as an ultimate principle.' However there is no difficulty in acknowledging that fallen humans do abuse truth. 'A Christian account of human nature accepts the capacity of the self for self-deception and its readiness to use strategies of manipulation.'[12] From one perspective postmodern theorists have a strong doctrine of sin!

Truth is incredible?

But in our culture the idea of an over all truth; of a story or philosophy which is the key to all our stories, is for many simply incredible. Perhaps the most famous definition of the 'postmodern' is given by Jean Francois Lyotard. 'Simplifying to the extreme I define "postmodern" as incredulity towards metanarratives.'[13] But in the same work Lyotard gave a clue to the source of his reasoning. 'The nineteenth and twentieth centuries have given us as much terror as we can take.'[14]

In other words, it is the appalling violence done in the name of truth, religious or not, in recent history, which has led to our culture's great suspicion of truth. It is the abuse of truth which has led to truth's apparent demise. And at a time when religious men, absolutely certain of the truth of their beliefs, fly airliners into towers packed full of their fellow human beings – believing that their suicides guarantee them instant access to Paradise; we should take seriously our culture's nervousness about religious certainty.

In one sense the new front line has a far better understanding of sin than the old front line. Of course I know that postmoderns don't really believe in sin. But they do know that humans abuse truth.

Postmodernism says, 'Truth cannot really be known'. It is either a distortion or a construct. At best it is fluid, good enough for now, but always up for grabs.

Christianity says, 'We are created for truth, but we run from it!' Here is the good news on the new front line.

- We are made in the image of God.
- Made like God for a relationship with God.
- A speaking and listening God creates speaking and listening people.
- Our words responding to God's words.

Here is the bad news on the new front line.

- We are a fallen race – evading truth, running from it or distorting it.
- We have exchanged the truth about God for a lie.
- We have loved darkness rather than light.[15]
- And if we say we have no sin we deceive ourselves and the truth is not in us.[16]

There is work to do on the New Front Line. We need

- A theology of language
- Nuanced disciplines of interpretation
- Greater recognition of the diverse genres of Scripture as a God-given polyphony complementing not contradicting
- A philosophy of Scripture as 'speech acts', varied acts of communication, not just propositions
- Sustained argument portraying Scripture as the trustworthy communication of a trustworthy God

Much of this work is being done, and I commend the work of John Goldingay[17], Anthony Thiselton[18], Kevin Vanhoozer[19], Tim Ward[20], John Webster[21], Nicholas Wolterstorff[22] and others.

But there is one thing needed more than a better Christian philosophy of knowledge. It is the promise of redemption. What postmoderns need most is not a better theory of truth, but to be set free from the power of sin, which makes us run from the truth.

Postmoderns need Scripture, because Scripture reveals Christ, 'The Truth' who says 'You will know the truth and the truth will make you free.' 'For if the Son makes you free, you will be free indeed.'[23]

Our response to scriptural truth

We have been focussing on the defense of Scripture on today's cultural front lines. That has a potential danger: that we start to think of Scripture as the subject we have to understand, which we address, rather than the voice we have to obey. Let Gordon Fee bring this section to its conclusion.

'Come to the text with an absolute conviction that it is God's Word: that here God speaks and we listen … The reason we must learn to do good exegesis is precisely because we are passionate to hear and obey.'[24]

B. Scriptural Truth from the Centre

In my first section I pointed out a vital distinction between our defense of Scripture – on today's cultural front line – and the central theological reasons why we recognize and submit to God's authority through Scripture. Now it is time to rehearse those reasons and to address 'Truth at the Centre'.

Christ is the centre of Scripture, as Francis Watson says: 'The writings of both Testaments converge on the figure of Jesus and on the triune divine identity disclosed in Jesus, and this convergence is the basis of their authority and trustworthiness.'[25]

As soon as we approach Christ as the Truth at the centre we discover an unavoidable interdependence between Christ himself – the incarnate Word of God – and Scripture the written Word of God. You cannot have one without the other.

If the argument is necessarily circular, it is not so much a closed circle as an open circle. 'Scripture, when rightly interpreted leads to Christ; Christ can be properly known only through Scripture.'[26] Each opens up the other. The more I am attracted to Christ, the more I turn to Scripture. The more I study Scripture, the more I discover Christ. And this is necessarily so because, ultimately, no external criterion can validate Scripture.

Lesslie Newbigin, commenting on the prologue to John's Gospel, described the challenge of evangelism in this way. The evangelist has to start with some common ground. Some basis in culture from which Christ can be preached. But Christ is the basis on which all cultures are judged. 'In the beginning was the Word'. So Christ is, 'The primal truth by which all else has to be confronted and questioned. That which in the end must be accepted as the beginning of all explanations.'[27]

On the old front line Enlightenment rationality or reason was treated as the ultimate judge. But as John Webster says, 'God is not summoned into the presence of reason: reason is summoned before the presence of God.'[28] How is that presence encountered? – 'The revelatory presence of God is set forth in Holy Scripture.'

Does this mean that the Christian case for Scriptural authority is based on some form of special pleading? Only if we believe that fallen human reason acts as a sort of accessible spectators' gallery, which provides a detached 50/50 vision of what is true.

And if we fight mainly on the new frontier, it is because hardly anybody holds that naïve perspective on reason any more. We now know that all truth is received through faith. For once the postmoderns and the premoderns agree. 'I believe in order to understand' (Anselm, Augustine, etc.).

All truth is perspectival. There is no spectators' gallery, no view from nowhere. Truth is acted on by faith.

At this point in the argument many postmoderns make a leap and say 'all truth is therefore relative' but the logic does not follow. A perspectival approach is not relativism. It does not deny revelation. And revelation does not depend on where we stand. It depends upon God's willingness to give it, and our willingness to receive it!

All truths may be perspectival, but all perspectives do not grant the same view. So find the perspective which shows the whole. Find the best place to stand! And that takes us to Scripture. 'Scripture is the place to stand when one wants to be in God's presence and learn of Him. Through the Bible we can orient ourselves to the objective revelation that has been given, and through the Spirit enter into it personally and dynamically.'[29]

Think with me for a moment about how you came to faith. At a key moment in the process Christ was preached, perhaps just through a personal testimony, but whether the Bible was quoted or not, the Christ of Scripture was preached.

As a result

- You came to faith in Christ
- You began to grow in your faith
- You started to trust Scripture

As Scripture became central to your faith in Christ you learned the arguments for trust in Scripture.

Few of us come to faith on the basis of believing an apologetic about Scripture. We are more likely to come to trust Scripture through conversion to Christ.

Many of us then learned the classic argument. I remember sitting at a Theological Students Fellowship meeting at university when John Stott taught us through it.

- Christ is our Lord – our authority
- He lived under the authority of OT Scripture
- His view of Scripture should be ours
- He commissioned his apostles
- He promised them the Spirit

This is a simple outline of the classical evangelical argument for trust in the authority and inspiration of Old and New Testaments, with Christ as the key to both. That is a perfectly reasonable argument, but there is much more. For a moment let us explore the relationship between Christ and Scripture.

His incarnate life was formed by OT Scripture

He was obedient to its commands. Both when tempted by the Devil and in his disputes with Pharisees or Saducees he quoted it as his authority. But above all he was shaped by its story. Israel's story becomes his story. God's purposes through Israel become his purposes. En route to Jerusalem he says, *I must be on my way for it is impossible for a prophet to be killed outside of Jerusalem.*[30] His cleansing of the temple re-enacts the destruction of the temple by the Babylonians, as he echoes Jeremiah's prediction of that event, and continually reapplies Scripture to his own calling.[31] The Old Testament Scriptures shape his life and ministry.

He was not only shaped by Old Testament Scripture ...

He fulfilled OT Scripture

You know his words. Teaching on the mountain, *I have come to fulfil the law and the prophets* (Matthew 5:17); as they arrest him, *Let the Scriptures be fulfilled* (Mark 14:49); on the road to Emmaus, *He interpreted to them the things about himself in all the Scriptures* (Luke 24:27); and in John, *These are the Scriptures that talk about me* (John 5:39).

He was the fulfillment, because otherwise the Old Testament was a story without an ending. Prophecies, dashed hopes, styles and traditions hanging loosely like a set of cut wires were all brought together in Jesus. Tom Wright put it this way, 'When Paul declares that the Messiah died for our sins according to the Scriptures he means that the entire scriptural story, the great drama of God's dealing with Israel, came together when the young Jew from Nazareth was nailed up by the Romans and left to die.'[32] When the entire scriptural story came together – the New Testament was created!

Jesus Created NT Scripture

The New Testament is the Old Testament fulfilled in Christ. 'As Jesus cannot be understood apart from Jewish Scripture; Jewish Scripture cannot be understood apart from Jesus.'[33]

In fulfilling the Old Testament Scriptures Jesus provides the model for the NT writers

The authority of the New Testament lies not just in Christ's commission to the apostles and his promise of the Spirit to remind them and guide them into truth. It was his example in fulfilling the Scriptures, which gave them the key to interpreting the Scriptures as they wrote. 'It was the conviction that God's purposes had been and were being fulfilled in Messiah Jesus that gave Paul the hermeneutical clue to read and understand the Scriptures.'[34]

The same can be said of Matthew, of the writer of Hebrews, and the rest. So Christ is indeed the key to all Scripture. *Long ago God spoke to our ancestors in many and various ways by the prophets, but in these last days, he has spoken to us by a Son, whom he appointed heir of all things.*[35]

And if Christ is the centre and key to Scripture, there follows, not so much a circular argument, but a spiraling argument. 'An adequate doctrine of Scripture depends circularly on the very doctrines that Scripture helps establish.'[36] So what can the doctrines Scripture reveals about Christ teach us about Scripture?

The Incarnation

As we have seen, we have access to no spectators' gallery overlooking the universe. But we do not need one. We did not have to step out of our perspectival skins to know truth. Christ stepped in. And all we need to do is to look through his eyes. 'In order to obtain a

God's eye view – we merely need to hold true to the narratives which identify Jesus and organize the rest of our beliefs accordingly.'[37]

Christ, by the Spirit, provides the perspective we need. 'The Holy Spirit's gift of wisdom gives us "an exhaustive view from on high which makes our perspective that of the Trinity." This is to be sure seeing in a mirror dimly (1 Cor. 13:12), and one day we shall see better, but it is sight none the less.'[38] When we evangelize, we invite people to look at the world, including themselves, through Christ's eyes.

But the incarnation teaches us to have confidence in the hermeneutical task as well; it instructs us about Scripture and culture. 'Take with utmost seriousness the culture-conditioned nature of Scripture without accepting that it is culture-determined. This is grounded ultimately in the incarnation.'[39] Just as the incarnate Son of God became a human of a particular culture at a particular time, but still is the source of salvation for all cultures at all times, so the Scriptures are products of the different cultures in which they were written, but also carry the Word of God to all cultures and times.

The Cross

But what can the cross teach us about Scripture?

That Scripture is an offence. 'The incarnation of the Son of God, in a world of sin, leads to the cross.'[40] The one whose life was shaped by Scripture was sent to the cross. The message of Scripture was and remains an offence to many. Paul understood this well. Where is the debater of this age? he asked. The Old Testament fulfilling message of the cross was a stumbling block, foolishness. But he also knew without doubt that God decided, through the foolishness of our proclamation, to save those who believe.

We must not become anti-intellectual. But in any age, the scriptural message will be seen as intellectually offensive.

The Resurrection

But the resurrection brings better news. For it enables us to see Scripture as a story of promises fulfilled. Jesus was *raised on the third day in accordance with the Scriptures.*[41] He fulfilled the whole scriptural story. As a consequence *in him every one of God's promises is a Yes.*[42]

In the resurrection Christ was validated. 'The divine act of raising Jesus from the dead was an unconditional validation of everything that he was in his incarnate life on earth, the teaching as much as the saving efficacy of Christ.'[43] Alec Motyer makes a crucial point. Christ's resurrection was the Father's validation of all that he was and taught. To say that Christ is the centre of Scripture is not just to say that doctrines about Christ are the centre of Scripture. It is to say that Christ's Scripture-shaped life is at the centre of Scripture, that there is no possibility of separating doctrine and ethics. That the Christ of Scripture requires a Christ-shaped life in his followers.

And for that he gave us the gift of the Spirit.

The gift of the Holy Spirit

Given under the inspiration of the Spirit, the Scriptures are first fruits. The first part of the final harvest which is to come. The Holy Spirit is – 'The certain evidence that the (God's) future has dawned, and the absolute guarantee of its final consummation.'[44] In the same way Scripture – is given as 'certain evidence' and as an 'absolute guarantee' of God's future. Sufficient truth to trust now, and sufficient power to live the truth now. Scripture is both a gift of truth and a promise of power.

The Challenge of Scripture

I set out to provide good reasons for trust in Scripture. But as I conclude, I want to face us with the challenge of Scripture. Which, more often than not, is disorientating! 'The gospel is good news because it is God's act of disorienting goodness.'[45]

Scripture is disorientating, because we are not very good at grace. We tend to turn it into law. With that law we are often hard on ourselves and harder on others. *But when the goodness and loving kindness of God our Saviour appeared he saved us ... according to his mercy.*[46] That is disorienting goodness. It is one thing to trust in Scripture. It is another to take its central message for granted.

The character of Scripture, centred upon God's gracious gift of his Son, is truth that expresses mercy. It calls us to a generous orthodoxy.[47] Orthodoxy – a unity based around Scripture, plus the creeds and the commandments as universally recognised distillations of Scripture. Generous – seeking unity and partnership with all those who share that Scripture-based centre of the faith. Not just with those who share our terminology or tradition.

The greatest divide in the Church today is between those who believe in the historic truths of the faith both doctrine and ethics – and those who do not. Shaped by Christ's truth, which expresses Christ's mercy, and by his generosity to us. Let us stand at the centre with all those believe, what Scripture teaches.

Notes

1. John Stott, *Evangelical Truth* (Leicester: Inter Varsity Press, 1999) p.56.
2. David Bebbington, *Evangelicalism in Modern Britain* (London: Routledge, 1993) ch.1.
3. 1 Corinthians 15:12 – 19
4. Peter Hicks, *Evangelicals and Truth* (Leicester: Apollos, 1998) p.11.
5. Richard Rorty, *Contingency, Irony and Solidarity* (Cambridge: Cambridge University Press, 1989) p. 4f.
6. Friedrich Nietzche, quoted in Anthony Thiselton, *Interpreting God and the Postmodern Self* (Edinburgh: T & T Clark, 1995) p.5.
7. George Steiner, *Real Presences* (London: Faber and Faber, 1989) p.4.
8. Jacques Derrida, *Of Grammatology* (Baltimore: Johns Hopkins University Press, 1976) p.148.
9. Richard Ashcroft, in an internet interview.
10. Kenneth Gergen, *Invitation to Social Construction* (London: Sage, 1999) p.2.

11. Jon Snyder, foreword to Gianni Vattimo, *The End of Modernity* (Cambridge: Polity, 1988) p.xii.

12. Anthony Thiselton, *Interpreting God and the Postmodern Self* (Edinburgh: T&T Clark, 1995) pp.13–14.

13. Jean Francois, *The Postmodern Condition* (Manchester: Manchester University Press, 1984) p.xxiv.

14. Ibid., p.62.

15. John 3:19.

16. 1 John 1:8.

17. John Goldingay, *Models for Scripture* (Carlisle: Paternoster, 1994) *Models for Interpreting Scripture* (Carlisle: Paternoster, 1995).

18. Anthony Thiselton, 'Authority and Hermeneutics', in Philip E. Satterthwaite and David. F. Wright (eds.), *A Pathway into Holy Scripture* (Grand Rapids: Eerdmans, 1994).

19. Timothy Ward, *Word and Supplement* (Oxford: Oxford University Press, 2002).

20. Kevin Vanhoozer, *Is There a Meaning in This Text?* (Leicester: Apollos, 1998); *First Theology* (Leicester: Apollos, 2002).

21. John Webster, *Holy Scripture* (Cambridge: Cambridge University Press, 2003).

22. Nicholas Wolterstorff, *Divine Discourse* (Cambridge: Cambridge University Press, 1995).

23. John 8:31, 36.

24. Gordon Fee, *Listening to the Spirit in the Text* (Grand Rapids: Eerdmans, 2000) pp.14, 15.

25. Frances Watson, 'An Evangelical Response', in Paul Helm and Carl Trueman (eds.), *The Trustworthiness of God* (Grand Rapids: Eerdmans, 2002) p.288.

26. Alister McGrath, *A Passion for Truth* (Leicester: Apollos, 1996) p.54.

27. Lesslie Newbigin, *The Light Has Come* (Grand Rapids: Eerdmans, 1989) p.2.

28. John Webster, *Holiness* (London: SCM Press, 2003) p.17.

29. Clark Pinnock, *The Scripture Principle* (London: Hodder and Stoughton, 1992) pp.163–64.
30. Luke 13:33.
31. See N. T. Wright, *Jesus and the Victory of God* (London: SPCK, 1996) pp.413–28.
32. Tom Wright, *What St. Paul Really Said* (Oxford: Lion, 1997) p.49.
33. R. W. Moberley, *The Bible, Theology and Faith* (Cambridge: Cambridge University Press, 2000) p.51.
34. James Dunn, *The Theology of Paul the Apostle* (Edinburgh: T & T Clark, 1998) p.173.
35. Hebrews 1:1–2.
36. Telford Work, *Living and Active* (Grand Rapids: Eerdmans, 2002).
37. Bruce Marshall, *Trinity and Truth* (Cambridge: Cambridge University Press, 1999) p.169.
38. Marshall, *op. cit.* p.169.
39. Jeremy Begbie; unpublished paper.
40. Miroslav Volf, *Exclusion and Embrace* (Nashville: Abingdon Press, 1996) p.25.
41. 1 Corinthians 15:4.
42. 2 Corinthians 1:20.
43. Alec Motyer, *Look to the Rock* (Leicester: Inter Varsity Press, 1996) p.21.
44. Gordon Fee, *God's Empowering Presence* (Peabody: Hendrickson, 1994) p.806.
45. John Webster.
46. Titus 3:4–5.
47. Stanley Grenz, *Renewing the Centre* (Grand Rapids: Baker, 2000) ch.10.

Chapter 5

The Bible in a Postmodern Age

David Peterson

A. Scriptural Sufficiency Explained

The perfection of Scripture

Orthodox Christians have traditionally affirmed the perfection of Scripture in terms of its *infallibility*, its *supreme authority* and its *sufficiency* for bringing people to a saving knowledge of God. But over the last two centuries there has been a progressive decline in such beliefs. What is now called modernism was a movement that attempted to subject the great bulk of Western intellectual and religious traditions to 'the canons of scientific reason'.[1] Postmodernism has radicalized this whole approach, challenging the supremacy of scientific reason and speaking of many 'truths'. As Graham Cray has pointed out, Western consumer society effectively reduced commitment to *any* worldview 'to something parallel to a supermarket shopping exercise, where "the Truth" was increasingly reduced to "my truth".'[2] In such a context, how can we affirm the uniqueness of Scripture and its truthfulness?

Infallibility

Timothy Ward discusses the notion of infallibility in the first chapter of *Fanning the Flame* – the resource book for this conference. He argues from Isaiah 55:11 (NRSV) that God's Word will infallibly perform the purpose for which he sent it:

> *so shall my word be that goes forth from my mouth;*
> *it shall not return to me empty,*
> *but it shall accomplish that which I purpose,*
> *and succeed in the thing for which I sent it.*

The truthfulness of the Bible and the effectiveness of its various parts to accomplish God's purpose are directly related to the *trustworthiness* and *sovereignty* of God himself. As Martin Luther said, 'A man's word is a little sound that flies into the air and soon vanishes; but the Word of God is greater than heaven and earth, yea greater than death and hell, for it forms a part of the power of God and endures everlastingly.'[3]

Authority

Paul Gardner considers the authority of Scripture in the second chapter of *Fanning the Flame*. Once again, he links a claim about the Bible to the character of God. Biblical authority is rooted in the authority of God himself: 'this Book, a gracious gift from God to his people, is treated as authoritative because the author, God, does not lie (Titus 1:2).'[4] Locating the authority of Scripture in God as the ultimate author necessitates a careful study of what he caused to be written, using the best tools available. But then, if we are to take the authority of this book seriously, it means submission to the revelation God has given and obedience to his words.

Sufficiency

So why do we need to speak about the sufficiency of Scripture in the light of these affirmations? Simply because there have always been those who could affirm the authority of Scripture, and even its infallibility, yet effectively treat the Bible as inadequate. Some have done this by focussing on the need for *tradition* to supplement, or even interpret Scripture. Many have emphasised the need for *reason* to modify and reapply what Scripture teaches. Some have taken *experience* as a source of new revelation or have allowed it to influence the way they interpret the Bible.

I want to look at these issues in the second part of this paper. But first I want to consider in what sense the Bible speaks of its own sufficiency. There can be no better starting point than an examination of 2 Timothy 3:15–17 (NIV).

The sufficiency of Scripture according to 2 Timothy 3:15–17

Sufficient for salvation

Paul reminds Timothy how from infancy he had known the Holy Scriptures,[5] *which are able to make you wise for salvation through faith in Christ Jesus.* This would include what we call the Old Testament, but possibly also apostolic documents which were soon regarded by the earliest Christians as having equal authority and status as 'Holy Scripture' (cf. 2 Peter 3:15–16). The claim that the Old Testament can *make you wise for salvation through faith in Christ Jesus* is consistent with the teaching of Jesus himself (e.g. Luke 24:27, 44–49; John 5:39–40). It is also consistent with the pattern of preaching recorded in the early chapters of Acts. Paul himself explains the gospel with constant reference to the Old Testament and its promises.

The writings of both Testaments *converge* on the figure of Jesus and on the triune God disclosed in Jesus. When we meet God through the Scriptures, their authority is confirmed for us experientially, in a direct and personal way. More specifically, Scripture as a whole provides a wisdom about salvation that is contrary to ordinary human thinking about religion. It shows us why we all need salvation and insists that God is the only one who can provide it. Salvation is not possible by doing good works or by being pious, as most people imagine, but only through faith in Christ and what he has accomplished for us. The sacred writings that form the canon of our Bible are *sufficient for salvation* inasmuch as they enable us to know Christ as the only Saviour and Lord of all and to turn to him in repentance and faith.

This means that the Bible should play an essential part in all genuine evangelism, whether we offer people portions of Scripture to read for themselves or we teach it to them publicly or one to one. Not every part of the Bible will be as clear and useful for evangelism as some others. But however we convey biblical teaching to unbelievers, we may be assured that the Holy Scriptures are sufficient to make them *wise for salvation through faith in Christ Jesus.* We may need to answer various questions and seek to persuade them. We will certainly need to pray for the Holy Spirit to give them understanding and to soften their hearts. But we can be confident in the sufficiency of the Scriptures to convert people. Indeed, we must beware of downplaying the Scriptures in our evangelistic efforts, giving the impression that we have little trust in the effectiveness of God's word to convict and change people, whether young or old.

At the same time, we must avoid thinking that we have to prove the inspiration and authority of Scripture as a preliminary to effective evangelism. Our aim should simply be to introduce people to the Lord Jesus in and through the Scriptures. Of course, there will come a time when the character of biblical inspiration and authority is questioned. Paul gives some guidance in the very next verse about the way we can respond.

God-breathed

> *All Scripture is God-breathed and is useful for teaching, rebuking, correcting and training in righteousness, so that the man of God may be thoroughly equipped for every good work (2 Timothy 3:16).*

The character of Scripture as God-breathed makes it useful and thoroughly effective for a range of things beyond salvation through faith in Christ.

The traditional rendering (*all Scripture is inspired by God*, RSV, NRSV) can give the impression that 'the writers of Scripture were helped, nudged and motivated by God to produce better and truer writing than they could ever have produced on their own.'[6] But the Greek word *theopneustos* implies that God has actually 'breathed out' Scripture, rather than inspiring the writers in the ordinary English sense of that word. Hence the NIV, *all Scripture is God-breathed* (*breathed out by God*, ESV).

This term recalls the Old Testament idea that God's word has creative power. In some contexts, such as Psalm 33:6, *the breath of his mouth* is a parallel to *the word of the Lord*:

> *By the word of the Lord the heavens were made,*
> *and all their host by the breath of his mouth.*

God sovereignly worked through the whole process by which the biblical documents were written, edited and collected together as the canon of Scripture.

The meaning of the term 'God-breathed' can be further defined by looking at the phenomenon of Scripture itself. Inspiration includes the idea that God spoke directly to prophets and apostles, giving them specific warnings and promises or detailed instructions about what to do. It also includes the notion that God superintended their writing down of these things, their own responses to historical situations and their own reflections on the world and their experiences of it.

As Tim Ward rightly argues, God worked *'concursively'*, that is 'with, in and through the thoughts and character of the human writer.'[7] Scripture is both human and divine: the writers *spoke from God as they were carried along by the Holy Spirit* (2 Peter 1:21 NIV, ESV). Because of God's supreme knowledge, power and trustworthiness, the product is uniquely 'the Word of God'. The God who is able to bring about revelatory events has ensured that some of the people involved in those events have been able to interpret and record them correctly for us.

Sufficient for Christian life and ministry

Since Scripture is God-breathed, it is uniquely *useful* for teaching, rebuking, correcting and training in righteousness. It provides sound doctrine and convicts heresy. It also corrects improper behaviour and educates positively in righteousness.[8] It will therefore fully equip Timothy as *the man of God* for the work that has been given to him. In the Pastoral Epistles, *man of God* appears to be a technical term for Timothy as a Christian leader (cf. 1 Timothy 6:11).

Verse 17 actually indicates that the ultimate purpose of Scripture's inspiration is to provide knowledge and direction for Christian ministry. So Scripture is sufficient for Timothy's work as an evangelist, as a corrector of false teaching and as an enabler of Christian growth. The utility of Scripture flows out of its inspiration. But the expression 'thoroughly equipped' implies *sufficiency*, not just utility. Nothing else is needed to make Timothy effective in his ministry. By implication, nothing else will be necessary for the believers to whom he ministers.

In contemporary terms, this must mean that the Bible will play an essential part in all genuine Christian ministry. It will be the basis and reference point for all doctrinal and ethical debates. It will be the means of refuting error. It will be the essential tool for equipping the saints for the work of ministry and for promoting Christian maturity (cf. Ephesians 4:11–16). It will be the inspiration for God-honouring prayer and praise, determining what we do when we meet together. It will guide the counsellor, the church planter and the denominational leader who wants to glorify God and promote his agenda in the churches. It will be at the centre of theological education, not just one subject amongst many, but determining the way other subjects are taught and ministers are prepared for their task. We would promote a godly revolution in our churches if we took 2 Timothy 3:15–17 seriously!

The finality of God's revelation in Christ

When we affirm the sufficiency of Scripture, we must include in our thinking the idea that God has fully and finally spoken to us *through his Son*. This is precisely the way the writer of Hebrews puts it:

> *Long ago God spoke to our ancestors in many and various ways by the prophets, but in these last days he has spoken to us by a Son. (Hebrews 1:1–2 NRSV)*

So the sufficiency of Scripture is linked to *Christology* – who Jesus Christ is as the ultimate revelation of God and his will – and to *eschatology* – the fact that we are living in 'these last days' before Christ returns.

The writer goes on to warn that we cannot escape God's judgement if we neglect the message of salvation which was *declared at first through the Lord* and *attested to us by those who heard him* (2:3). Already it is clear that the final revelation given through the Son is *mediated by his chosen witnesses.* Here we have the beginning of the concept of a New Testament, written by those divinely authorized to explain the significance of the Christ event.

Hebrews has a strong theology of God continuing to speak to his people under the New Covenant through the prophetic Scriptures. They have been fulfilled in Christ, who has brought every promise and provision of God to perfection. The writer feels compelled to *draw out the meaning* of what Christ has done and to warn and encourage his readers on this basis. But the whole focus of the book is on responding to what God has already said and done in Christ, not on new revelations.[9]

The sufficiency of Scripture according to Anglican formularies

Article 6

Article 6 of the Thirty-nine Articles echoes 2 Timothy 3:15 in declaring the sufficiency of the Holy Scriptures for salvation:

> *Holy Scripture containeth all things necessary to salvation; so that whatsoever is not read therein, nor may be proved thereby, is not required of any man, that it should be believed as an article of the Faith, or be thought requisite or necessary for salvation.*

This was a fundamental principle of the Reformation because the medieval church had taught and practised the view that Scripture was not sufficient, but had to be 'supplemented and interpreted by the traditions which the Church possesses and has preserved from the beginning.'[10]

This Reformation principle was designed to deliver God's people from spiritual tyranny, setting them free from the necessity to believe in anything that could not be established from Scripture.[11]

The ordination vow

The Prayer Book service for the ordination of priests questions whether the candidate is persuaded that 'the holy Scriptures contain sufficiently all Doctrine required of necessity for eternal salvation through faith in Jesus Christ' and whether the ordinand is determined 'out of the said Scriptures to instruct the people committed to your charge, and to teach nothing, as required of necessity to eternal salvation, but that which you shall be persuaded may be concluded and proved by the Scripture'.[12]

Scripture the supreme authority in every area

You will sometimes hear it said that the Prayer Book articles and ordinals only bind Anglicans to believe in the sufficiency of Scripture for salvation. By implication, many secondary issues are excluded. However, it is important to notice the extent to which Scripture is the supreme authority in regard to other matters, in at least eighteen of the articles.[13] The three creeds are to be received and believed 'because they may be proved by most certain warrants of Holy Scripture'. The doctrine of the Church is also tested by and made subject to the Word of God. Certain doctrines are condemned because they are repugnant to Holy Scripture. The doctrine of the sacraments and questions of church order and discipline are formulated on the basis of Scripture. Even questions about the relations of Church and State are discussed in the light of Scripture.

If we are to be faithful to the doctrinal standard and practice of the Thirty-nine Articles of Religion, the Book of Common Prayer and the Ordinal, we should be constantly re-assessing and reforming ourselves in the light of Holy Scripture. It is the historic Anglican way of doing theology to make Scripture the final court of appeal in every matter. Scripture's sufficiency for salvation has to do with doctrinal and ethical matters. The exposition and application of Scripture in the local church should therefore be the outstanding characteristic of contemporary Anglican ministry.

Conclusion

The infallibility, authority and sufficiency of Scripture are related to the character of our God – his trustworthiness, sovereignty and wisdom. Scripture is not intended to provide knowledge about every field of study or interest, but only the knowledge that God wants us to have for our salvation, growth to maturity in Christ and effectiveness in ministry to one another and to an unbelieving world. The sufficiency of Scripture lies in its ability to do just that.

B. Scriptural Sufficiency Applied

I mentioned that there are broadly three ways in which the sufficiency of Scripture has been challenged – in connection with tradition, reason and experience. I want to examine these in turn, but first to say a little more about the sufficiency of Scripture to make us *wise for salvation through faith in Christ Jesus* (2 Timothy 3:15).

Salvation and the uniqueness of Christ

This has tremendous relevance for one of the most fundamental debates going on amongst professing Christians today: is Jesus Christ the only way to eternal salvation?

Salvation through any sincerely held belief?

Postmodernism has revitalised the age-old question about truth in other religions and about the genuineness of any sincerely held belief. Religious tensions in the world today make some Christian apologists insist that we stop talking about the uniqueness of Christ and abandon any attempts to evangelise people of other faiths. Sometimes the biblical teaching about Christ as the only way is totally dismissed. Sometimes it is modified so that genuine believers in other religions are said to have implicit faith in the anonymous Christ. Sometimes special exemptions are argued.

Much could be said about this issue. I simply want to remind you that our claim about the sufficiency of Scripture will really put us to the test on this point. Here, perhaps, more than anywhere else, we may be tempted to capitulate to the spirit of the age.

Acts 4:12 in context

Key texts in any debate must be carefully explained in their contexts. Take Acts 4:12 as an example: *There is salvation in no one else, for there is no other name under heaven given among mortals by which we must be saved* (NRSV). This is directed to the rulers and elders of Israel, who had seen the Lord Jesus and heard him teach. They had witnessed the healing of the crippled man in Christ's name, but were seeking to prevent Peter and John from preaching him to the people. There are no exceptions to the apostolic claim, even for the audience of Jews and proselytes on the Day of Pentecost. All must repent and be baptised in the name of Jesus Christ (Acts 2:38 – 39). Indeed, salvation in 'the name' of Christ implies a knowledge of the significance of his name and calling upon him explicitly as Lord and Christ for the salvation proclaimed (cf. Acts 2:21, 36). There is no possibility for implicit faith in the anonymous Christ here.

Doctrine, Scripture and Tradition

Traditions evaluated by Scripture

The issue of tradition as a supplement to Scripture or even as a key to the interpretation of Scripture was at the heart of the Reformation in the sixteenth century. Our Anglican Reformers did not abandon every tradition, but maintained some because they were seen to be consistent with Scripture. These included the practice of infant baptism and episcopal government. But they argued that even well-established traditions must be constantly re-evaluated in the light of Scripture.[14]

The Church as 'a witness and a keeper of Holy Writ'

When the Reformers taught that Scripture is supreme over the Church, they meant that every belief and practice should be evaluated in the light of Scripture. Article 20 states that the Church is 'a witness and a keeper of Holy Writ'. This does not mean, as some have argued, that the Church has the authority to read the Bible in a new way for a new generation, since the Church 'gave birth' to the Scriptures. The Church itself was born through the preaching and teaching of the apostles, which was based on what we call the Old Testament. Apostolic teaching was soon written down and recognised as New Testament Scripture. The problem came when church traditions were given an equal status or allowed to determine the way Scripture was interpreted.

Nothing contrary to 'God's word written'

Article 20 insists that:

> The Church hath power to decree Rites or Ceremonies, and authority in Controversies of Faith; and yet it is not lawful for the Church to ordain any thing that is contrary to God's word written, neither may it so expound one place of Scripture that it be regugnant to another.

You will recognise the importance of this principle in debates that we are having at the moment, for example about homosexuality. It is 'God's Word written', in all its complexity and with all its perspectives, that must be properly evaluated. A passage like Romans 1 cannot be taken to speak with a different voice, as if the Bible contained many theologies and conflicting ethical judgements. I will have more to say about this shortly.

The fallibility of councils

Human attempts to explain and apply the Bible's teaching will always be fallible. Article 21 states that even General Councils of the Church may err because not all the participants 'be governed with the Spirit and Word of God'. Nevertheless, the challenge to any synod or committee must always be to gain a holistic view of Scripture on any topic and ultimately to sit under its authority, no matter how difficult that may be in the current climate.

So if we believe in the sufficiency of Scripture, this does not mean that we can do without creeds or councils or liturgies or traditions. It does mean that Scripture is supreme and that we are called in each generation to re-examine and re-apply its teaching with honesty and humility, being willing to live by it ourselves and calling others to do the same.

Reason, Scripture and Ethics

Using our minds

Human reason has an important part to play in the process of interpretation and application. God wants us to use our minds to *understand what the will of the Lord is* (Ephesians 5:17). He wants us to *be transformed by the renewing of our minds, so that you may discern what is the will of God – what is good and acceptable and perfect* (Romans 12:2). So theology is a rational discipline.

However, faith goes beyond reason, 'having access to truths and insights of revelation, which reason could not hope to fathom or discover unaided. Reason has the role of building upon what is known by revelation, exploring what its implications might be.'[15]

The problem comes when human reason is allowed to be the supreme authority and sit in judgement on Scripture. This has been the dominant approach since the so-called Enlightenment of the eighteenth century, particularly when scientific research appears to contradict Scripture or where new situations demand ethical judgements for which Scripture seems to give little guidance.

Yielding to divine revelation

'Revelation does not dishonour reason, but honours it by appealing to it with evidence, for to the spiritual, enlightened mind the Scriptures make a constant appeal.'[16] However, when the evidence has been examined, reason must yield to the superior authority of divine revelation. This applies as much to the apostolic testimony about the resurrection of Jesus as it does to the apostolic teaching about eternal judgement and Jesus being the only way of salvation.

Those who submit to revelation on these key issues sometimes still have problems submitting in other areas. For example, in ethical matters, such as the homosexuality debate, we are often told that medical and psychological evidence should lead us to reassess or move on from scriptural teaching. On issues such as euthanasia, we are told that the Bible has little to say and that we should make up our minds on the basis of contemporary evidence and argument. The apparent sophistication of our age makes people dismissive of biblical teaching. But in all such matters, we must search the Scriptures for specific teaching and for a divine framework to inform our thinking. Only then will we be able to evaluate current perspectives effectively.

Dealing with a variety of scriptural interpretations

Postmodernism has encouraged interpreters to believe that a variety of scriptural interpretations on a given topic is possible. God does not speak with one voice in Scripture and the perspectives and insights of individual commentators elicit a breadth of meaning for current application. So, for example, Walter Brueggemann, the Old Testament scholar has said:

> The great new fact of interpretation is that we live in our pluralistic context, in which many different interpreters, in many different specific contexts representing many different interests, are at work on textual (theological) interpretation. The old consensus about limits and possibilities of interpretation no longer holds. Thus interpretation is no longer done by a small, tenured elite, but interpretive voices and their very different readings of the texts come from many cultures in all parts of the globe, and from many sub-cultures even in Western culture.[17]

I am sure we could all endorse some of the positive implications of this. No longer can 'the small, tenured elite' of Western academics tell us how Scripture must be interpreted. Insights from various cultures and subcultures can open our eyes to new perspectives on Scripture. But the idea that 'consensus about limits and possibilities of interpretation no longer holds' is a total concession to postmodernism, and an abandonment of traditional views about the inspiration and unity of Scripture. It implies that God is not powerful enough to reveal his will in Scripture in a clear and discernible way.

Quite often, this approach involves an atomistic approach to biblical texts, with little regard for literary or theological context. Brueggemann himself acknowledges that in each of these rival interpretations there is in fact 'the advocacy of a vested interest, which may be highly visible or hidden.'[18]

Does this mean that there are no ways in which we can determine the original intention of the human authors? Is no interest-free interpretation possible? Does it mean, then, that God speaks to his people with different voices? Does he really want the Church to have conflicting views on important matters such as sexual ethics? Does he want the Bible to be manipulated to endorse varying opinions? Does the old Reformation belief that the Church may not 'so expound one place of Scripture that it be repugnant to another' have no significance any more?

God's character and purpose

Those who are committed to a biblical view of the sufficiency of Scripture cannot rest with the postmodern solution. As we have already noted, the sufficiency of Scripture is linked to the character and purpose of God in communicating with us. He does not say to his people, 'Seek me in chaos'. As Isaiah 49:19 declares, *I the Lord speak the truth, I declare what is right.* Those who believe this must give themselves energetically to discover the way different scriptural passages on a given topic can be read together, to reveal the mind of God.

So biblical theology is an important discipline for us to recover. This is the attempt to read the Bible holistically, seeking to discover how the various parts fit into the developing whole.

Experience, Scripture and the Holy Spirit

Experience as a resource for theology?

The idea that experience provides a *foundational resource* for Christian theology emerged very early in Church History and has surfaced many times since. It is an obvious characteristic of the postmodern era.[19] Theological liberals would argue that Christian theology is not based on special revelation from God in Scripture. The Bible is a collection of human responses to the experiences of Israel and the early Church. On this view, contemporary experiences may be just as valid as the biblical experiences as a way of knowing God and his will.

However, as Alistair McGrath has argued, if there is such a thing as special revelation from God in Scripture, this must provide 'a *framework* within which the ambiguities of experience may be interpreted.'[20]

McGrath points to the positive role given to experience in the thinking of Augustine and Luther. Yet Luther himself demonstrates how unreliable experience and feelings can be as guides to the presence and purpose of God. For example, the disciples at the time of the crucifixion must have felt that God had abandoned them. The Jewish authorities doubtless felt that God had vindicated their opposition to Jesus. But if they had understood the Scriptures and believed the predictions of Jesus, they would have known what a mighty act of salvation God was accomplishing through those tragic events.

An escape from reason and Scripture?

In the nineteenth century, 'many theologians regarded experienced-based theologies as providing an escape from the impasse of Enlightenment rationalism, or from difficulties relating to the alleged particularity of Christian revelation.'[21] We need to be aware that postmodernism encourages many to adopt similar solutions today. When experience becomes an independent source for our knowledge of God, it challenges, contradicts or ignores the revelation that God has given for all his people throughout time in the canon of Scripture.

At a popular level, this problem surfaces when people seek God's guidance through feelings, or convictions, or events in their lives. It surfaces when people make moral judgements on the basis of their experience of another person or situation. For example, someone at a conference on the biblical teaching about sexuality said to me, 'I am challenged by what you say, but I cannot condemn someone I know who is living in a homosexual relationship, because he is such a kind and considerate Christian. I would rather be right with my friend and wrong with Paul.'

New revelations by the Spirit?

Evangelicals have been particularly divided over the issue of contemporary prophetic revelations. Is God really in these phenomena and what is their significance? Paul expects that God will continue to 'reveal' to his people the implications of the gospel for their lives (e.g. Philippians 3:15; Ephesians 1:17). Such a disclosure might come through a prophetic ministry, during a Christian meeting (1 Corinthians 14:30), or through quiet reflection on the contents of the apostle's letters.[22] This work of the Holy Spirit has traditionally been called illumination, because it involves a better understanding of the revelation given to all in Christ, not new revelation in the sense of something unprecedented (cf. 2 Corinthians 4:6).

Indeed, Paul makes an important distinction between *his* prophetic authority as an apostle of Christ and the authority of the prophets ministering in the church at Corinth. He says, *Anyone who claims to be a prophet, or to have spiritual powers, must acknowledge that what I am writing to you is a command of the Lord. Anyone who does not recognize this is not to be recognized* (1 Corinthians 14:37 – 38 NRSV). The content and style of prophetic ministry in the congregation is to be tested by the definitive, written word of the apostle, which has the status of *a command of the Lord*. Scripture must be supreme in assessing both public and private 'revelations'.

Conclusion

Once again, I would affirm that the sufficiency of Scripture is related to the doctrine of God revealed in Scripture itself. God is trustworthy, sovereign and wise. He is able to communicate clearly and definitively to his people through his human agents and their written words.

The sufficiency of Scripture is a necessary doctrine because of the Bible's own teaching about humanity. We are rebellious and anxious to suppress or distort the truth in our own interests. Without a sufficient word from God, we are left to our own devices and the inevitable corruption that follows.

True Christian unity can only be found in confessing and living out *the faith that was once for all entrusted to the saints* (Jude 3; cf. Ephesians 4:1–6). This has been preserved for all generations of believers in the canon of Scripture. When the sufficiency of Scripture is doubted or denied, God's purpose for his Church is impeded (cf. Ephesians 4:12–13).

Notes

1. S. Williams, 'Towards Trust', in P. Helm & C. Trueman (ed.), *The Trustworthiness of God Perspectives on the Nature of Scripture* (Leicester: Apollos, 2002) p.219. Williams later describes the Reformation as giving 'freedom from the tyranny of the papacy', the Enlightenment 'freedom from the tyranny of the Bible', and postmodernity 'freedom from reason' (p.223)!
2. Graham Cray, 'Obeying the Truth in a Network Society: The Problem of Truth in a Changed Society', *Fanning the Flame: Bible, Cross and Mission* (Grand Rapids: Zondervan, 2003) p.68.
3. Martin Luther, 'Of God's Word' XLIV, in W. Hazlitt (trans.), *The Table Talk or Familiar Discourses of Martin Luther* (London: David Bogue, 1848) p.20.
4. Paul Gardner, 'Isn't It All a Matter of Interpretation? Scripture, Truth and Our World', *Fanning the Flame*, p. 47.
5. I assume Pauline authorship for the reasons argued by William D. Mounce, *Word Biblical Commentary Vol. 46 Pastoral Epistles* (Nashville: Nelson, 2000) pp.xlvi-cxxxvi.
6. Timothy Ward, 'The Bible, Its Truth and How It Works', *Fanning the Flame*, p.25.
7. Ward, 'The Bible, Its Truth and How It Works', p.26. If this idea is taken seriously, then the reader will take careful

account of 'the literary and contextual character of every biblical verse' and will ask where a verse fits in the course of God's progressive revelation (p. 27). Cf. Mounce, *Pastoral Epistles*, p. 566.

8. Following Mounce, *Pastoral Epistles*, p. 570.

9. This is even true in a passage like Hebrews 12:25–29, where the challenge to listen to 'the one who is speaking' refers back to the affirmation that God speaks through the Scriptures (12:5–6) and 'from heaven' through the victory of Christ (12:22–24).

10. W. H. Griffith Thomas, *The Principles of Theology: An Introduction to the Thirty-Nine Articles* (5th ed. rev.), (London: Church Book Room, 1963) p.120.

11. A belief in the sufficiency of Scripture rescues us from the tyranny of human traditions, the sinfulness of human reason and the fallibility of human experiences.

12. The ordination service in *The Alternative Service Book 1980* has a very much reduced and inadequate version of this question. It remains to be seen whether the new ordination service will strengthen the charge.

13. I am indebted to Griffith Thomas, *Principles of Theology*, p. 123, for what follows.

14. So, for example, the way we practice the Lord's Supper needs to be reviewed continually in the light of Scripture. We must be careful about reading Scripture in the light of our Anglican tradition or allowing our tradition as it has developed to have ultimate authority.

15. Alister McGrath, *Christian Theology: An Introduction* (2nd ed.) (Oxford: Blackwell, 1997) p.213.

16. Griffith Thomas, *Principles of Theology*, p.124.

17. Walter Brueggemann, *Theology of the Old Testament: Testimony, Dispute, Advocacy* (Minneapolis: Fortress, 1997) pp.61–62.

18. Brueggemann, *Theology of the Old Testament*, p.62.

19. Cf. Graham Cray, 'Obeying the Truth in a Network Society', p.73.

20. McGrath, *Christian Theology*, p.227 (my emphasis).
21. McGrath, *Christian Theology*, p.230.
22. Cf. P. T. O'Brien, *The Epistle to the Philippians: A Commentary on the Greek Text* (Grand Rapids: Eerdmans, 1991) pp.439–40.

Chapter 6

Getting the Message Out – the Bible

Christina Baxter

I am going to look at some themes from 1 Thessalonians chapter one.

While you were here on Saturday evening, and no doubt having some extremely helpful presentations, I was stuck in the most enormous traffic jam. I was here on Friday, but I went out at Saturday tea-time, and I was caught up in the traffic that wanted to look at the Blackpool Illuminations. And for more than three hours I had the opportunity to focus my eyes on the world to which we are commissioned to proclaim the gospel.

Not the world in other countries, but the world in this country. People of all different shapes and size, people out for a good night; people who do not know the love of God as it is in Christ Jesus. People who are desperately seeking for meaning in drink, and entertainment, and sex, and drugs. People for whom the Lord Jesus Christ died. If you are like me, you have only come to this Congress because you have in your heart God's passion for making the gospel known to this nation; because you have a great prayer desire that in our day we would see thousands and thousands of people turn back to the Lord Jesus Christ.

We have heard an enormous amount of theology, which has been brilliant, and an enormous amount of advice about difference circumstances in which we work and minister, and this brief talk is intended to think about how we can, together, allow the Word of God to go to every corner of our land, into the hearts and lives of girls and boys, women and men, into our institutions, our cities, inner cities and outer cities, into our suburbs and our countryside. I suppose if we were yet sure about how God is going to do that, we probably wouldn't be sitting here, but engaged in the task.

I believe that God has help for us in this passage from 1 Thessalonians. St Paul talks about the way that the Thessalonians came to faith, and he says in 1:8, *The word of the Lord has sounded forth from you, not only in Macedonia and Achaia, but in every place your faith in God has become known so that we have no need to speak of it.* Neither St Paul nor I are suggesting that we don't talk about God's love for people, but the word of the Lord has sounded forth like a trumpet in Thessalonica. I wonder why that was the case for them, and perhaps isn't always the case for us. What were they being and doing that perhaps we are not? What was the reason for this enormous spread of the gospel, moving so quickly from a church that was planted in a great hurry and remained weak, and few in numbers? How did it happen?

Well, St Paul says that the reason it happened was that *in spite of persecution you received the word with joy inspired by the Holy Spirit* (v. 6). I am going to ask you over coffee to do a little exercise. Perhaps you can find somebody you don't know, and you can tell them about a time recently when you received the Word of the Lord with joy, by the Holy Spirit.

I don't know about you, but I often think that the way in which we receive the Scriptures is multilayered. We have it in our everyday reading, in our worship; we read the whole of the Scriptures. But from time to time, God 'plants' something in our hearts and lives, and it becomes a wellspring to which we go again and again, even when we are listening to other passages. And my guess is that for most of us there may be one or two passages which have been a kind of pilot through the whole of our lives. Maybe it was the verse through which we came to faith. Or perhaps it's a passage through which God called us to work in the world or in the church. Or maybe it's some other key passage which God has just planted in our lives and said, 'Never go far away from this'. And those words have shaped our lives, made us who we are; they go on being the fixed point of God's word to us, his promise to us. And they have changed our whole lives. Between us, we have an enormous testimony to receiving the Word of God despite persecution, with joy, because of the work of the Holy Spirit.

I would love to tell you about some of the passages of the Old and New Testament that God has used in my life. The really big one was when God told me, through Joshua chapter 1, that *this book of the Law shall not depart out of your mouth, for you shall study to do all that is written in it. Then you will make your way successful* (Joshua 1:8). That passage has shaped everything I have done and been in the last forty years. And you will have stories like that to tell as well. And maybe one of the things we could well do today is to talk to people we don't know about the commonality of our faith, and the fact that God's word is in our lives by the power of the Holy Spirit, bringing us great joy despite persecution. And it is making a difference about where and how we live, what we make our priorities, even how we are. St Paul says that when the Word of God isn't just in our heads but in our hearts and our hands, and on our lips and in our lives, then the Word of God sounds forth in every place.

Now I am asking myself the question, what would make the Word of God sound forth form this place? What would make people write articles in the newspapers at the end of the Congress that were radically different from the ones at the beginning of the Congress? What would make that difference, I believe, is each and every one of us, individually but corporately, receiving the Word of God despite persecution and suffering, with joy, by the power of the Holy Spirit. And the thing that is going to carry conviction, is lives changed. So if before we came, people were saying that we evangelicals cannot live and work together, if what they see as we leave this Congress is people holding hands with one another, and absolutely determined for the sake of the gospel to stay together, to pray together, to suffer together, to struggle together, to dialogue together, and to come to a common mind about the Lord Jesus Christ and his purposes – that ought to hit the headlines. And if what we can say at the end of the

Congress is, as a result of what we've heard and how God has spoken to us, we're going to live more holy lives, we're going to live it in our personal lives, we've come to repent of some of the things we arrived thinking and doing and being, and God has shown us how we ought to be different in the future – and if we didn't only say that, but we did it – that would hit the headlines. People would notice that we are different, and the Word of God would sound out, from here into the places to which we go.

Now those aren't two illustrations I have drawn at random from an over-feverish imagination. Those are the two things that St. Paul talks about in 1 Thessalonians chapter 4. He says to them, there are two things that I want you to attend to, two places where I want the Word of God to burn like fire in your lives, and to change you.

The first is about holiness; 1 Thessalonians 4:1 – 8 is all about holiness. *God did not call us to impurity, but in holiness.* One of the hardest things I ever have to do, I think, is to pray a prayer that a mature and wonderful Christian woman taught me, which is that when I see sin in others I need to pray both for them and for me, repentance. I don't know about you, but I struggle sometimes with being a friend of sinners. The reason I struggle is that I am a sinful friend of sinners. I am not, as Jesus Christ was, the friend of sinners without sin. And my struggle to stand alongside those who I know are displeasing God is made harder because in my own heart those things are present as well.

So we are called to holiness. If we go away from this Congress and there is not a single way in which we can say that God has changed us, helped us to see that we should come to repentance, and we need to be more holy, together and individually, then is it any wonder that the Word of God does not sound out to our land?

The other concern of chapter four is Paul's talk about love of the brothers and sisters. He says that *you do not need to have anyone to write to you, because you yourselves have been taught by God to love one another. But we urge you beloved to do so more and more* (4:9 – 10). We wouldn't have come to Blackpool, of course, if we hadn't loved God, if we hadn't loved one another, and we hadn't had a gospel heart. We would have spent this weekend doing something much 'better' – I can think of a hundred things I would rather do than be in Blackpool for this Congress. But God would not let me out of it! God's love is poured out in our hearts. So, if there is love amongst us, St Paul says, *do so more and more* (v. 10). And of course it's very easy to urge ourselves to love one another, but loving one another is all about getting to know one another. It's all about finding out what the others think and say and do and how they are. It's about sharing their concerns. And before you leave this Congress, I beg you if you haven't done it already, find someone in the inner cities who is desperately struggling with ways to make the gospel known, and yet is living the gospel. And if you live in the inner cities, find someone from that most difficult missionary area, the leafy South, and find out how difficult it is to preach the gospel to those who are wealthy. And if you haven't done it already, find someone from Cumbria, or one of the other rural areas, and ask, what is it like to be a Christian in places where there has been such recent devastation through Foot and Mouth, and where the church is struggling to be a witness.

If we love one another already, *do so more and more.*

Now, why does Paul say all of these things? Because the Word of God sounds forth from the Christians in Macedonia because they received it with joy, in spite of persecution, by the Holy Spirit – but they also lived it. He says at the beginning of that passage of 1 Thessalonians, that when he preached the gospel it came *not only in word, but in power and the Holy Spirit and with full conviction, just as you know what kind of persons we proved to be among you for your sake. And you became imitators of us and of the Lord, for in spite of persecution you received the word with joy.* What was the thing that made the Word of God so convincing to the Thessalonians? Well, it was the work of the Holy Spirit, it was the power of God. But it was Paul among them, living the life of the crucified, giving himself away for them, letting his life be shaped by the shape of the cross, taking up his cross daily, and living a cruciform life – that life lived is the testimony that goes with the Word of God and which enables people to receive it. Now we have heard about that in some of our sessions, and we know it is true. People come to faith when they hear the Word of God preached, not only with lips but by the Holy Spirit in people's hearts, and by Christian people who live the gospel. And if we are concerned for this nation to turn back to Jesus Christ then maybe we ought to ask ourselves the question, are our lives shaped by the cross of Christ? Are our lives self-giving to one-another and to the world? Is the other person more important than me, or am I still clinging on to power and position, and all those other things that deny what we say because we do not live it. 'Be not only hearers of the word, but *be-ers* also' – I know James says 'do-ers', but it's another way of putting it. Live like Jesus, and that way the Word of God goes forward.

Now, the Archbishop of York asked us to keep silence last night, and there's a lot more I could say, but that's enough I think. So we are going to keep silence and think for a moment or two about what St Paul has said. God's desire is that the word sounds forth. He wants us to receive it with joy, by the power of the Holy Spirit. He wants us to live it in love for one another, and in holiness.

'Come, Holy Spirit of God. Fill our hearts with love for you and for holiness. Come, Holy Spirit of God, fill our hearts with love for one another, and for all our sisters and brothers in Christ. Come, Holy Spirit of God, and fill our hearts with love for your world, and for all the people for whom Christ died. Come, Holy Spirit of God. Amen.'

The Cross

Theme 2

Theme 2: The Cross

Peter Jensen, Anthony Thiselton
and Wallace Benn

For many of the delegates it was a surprise to discover that these talks were where the Congress first came alive. As Peter Jensen and Anthony Thiselton spoke they – like all the speakers – were projected on large screens either side of the stage, and it was clear to the audience from these vast close-ups that both of them, eminent scholars though they are, had tears in their eyes as they spoke. What only those close to them heard, as each listened to the other's paper, was that they were both murmuring, 'Oh, we need to hear this', over and again.

Wallace Benn's Conference Sermon at the Communion service was on the theme of the Cross, and this is the appropriate section of the book to record it. There was a moving and powerful summary talk on this theme by John Irvine, the Dean of Coventry Cathedral, which used extensive visual material of his home city and Cathedral. Sadly, that means it cannot adequately be reproduced in written form.

The Most Revd Dr Peter Jensen is Archbishop of Sydney

Canon Professor Anthony C. Thiselton is professor of Christian Theology at the University of Nottingham

The Rt Revd Wallace Benn is Bishop of Lewes

Chapter 7

The Atonement – the Heart of Our Message

Peter Jensen

The Just God – Good News, but Do We Want Him?

Here is some really good news: the Lord says, *I will never acquit the guilty* (Exodus 23:7). This means that the universe is not a morally chaotic jungle, where might is right and evil will triumph. There is one righteous God who rules over all things and, even though sin and evil may abound, that is not going to be the final state of things: *I will not acquit the guilty.* Here is a sentence full of hope and promise that God's good kingdom will come.

The fact that you are not exactly cheerful about this news shows that you have noted the catch. Good as it is to know that evil will not triumph, what if we are included amongst the guilty? In the light of God's known character and his known will for the human race, this seems more than certain. You do not need a God who never acquits the guilty. *You* need a God who acquits the ungodly. But what sort of God would that be?

We Dream of Freedom – but We Are in Slavery

Contemporary human beings dream of freedom: it is our great hope and our chief ambition. We want to be free of all outside influence;

we want to be so free that we can do whatever we please. The Bible knows nothing of utterly free human beings. It only knows of men and women in bondage to their lords. Jesus himself said: *Everyone who sins is a slave to sin* (John 8:34). That is, we have the status of a slave, unable to be free. The Bible says that we are enslaved by our fear of death, and with good reason. Death is not the natural end of life, an opening to the peace of oblivion. Death is the opening to judgement in which the law of God will condemn the sin of our hearts and tongues and lives: *The sting of death is sin, and the power of sin is the law* (1 Corinthians 15:56).

Death itself is God's judgement on our sinfulness, and the law of God reveals to our consciences, that beyond death there is a judgement with a God before whose justice we should quail. More, we are prey to the fashions of this world, mindlessly following the mob in its denial of God. More, we are spiritually captive, blinded by the god of this world, the prince of this world (Ephesians 2:1–3); and he holds the power of death (Hebrews 2:14). In the secularist West, unbelief is the great triumph of the evil one. The gospel that Jesus Christ is Lord remains God's answer.

The Freedom of Having a Good Lord – Jesus Christ

The freedom we need is the freedom of having a good Lord, one who will acquit the guilty *because* he is righteous. The essence of the Christian gospel is that Jesus Christ is that Lord. In a society which was so familiar with slavery, to preach Christ as Lord was to say that there was a new possibility open for human beings. The evil of slavery was compounded by having a bad master. The gospel offered all people a wonderful, kind and generous master; true freedom via slavery to the Lord. Your freedom was not that you could choose to do whatever you pleased, but that you were bound to a good master, who would choose what you *should* please. This Lord was Jesus Christ.

How Did the Lord Acquire You?

How did this Lord acquire you? Following the metaphor of slavery, the apostolic preachers tell us that he acquired his slaves through purchase, through redemption, through ransom. Our release from deadly bondage to the world and sin and the evil one and the fear of death has been accomplished by a great Lord. We, therefore, owe him everything which both the rights of purchase, *and* thankful hearts can bring him. Furthermore, and it is here of course that the language of ransom breaks its own boundaries, he did not purchase us with money, but through his own death. Again and again in the New Testament we discover the truly crucial point, the pivotal moment in our salvation is the death of Jesus Christ. His incarnation, his resurrection, his ascension – all these and more are essential to his work. But it is his death which is the key. It is no accident that the gospels give so much attention to his death and that Paul can say: *we preach Christ crucified* (1 Corinthians 1:23).

Up until now we were united to Adam, a real loser; we were members of a team doomed to relegation, to annihilation. By the power of his Spirit, Christ now unites us to himself, so that all the blessings of God are, and are to be, ours. Listen to five of these blessings.

Five Blessings of Christ's Redemption

Release from bondage

First of all, we have been released from bondage to the evil one. We are now in Christ's kingdom, the kingdom of light. We were in the kingdom of darkness – the kingdom where Satan ruled by keeping us in the dark and unable to escape – but the Lord has raided the powers of darkness and has released us. His victory was for our benefit. How did he accomplish this? Was it by 'paying' Satan? Not so: our redemption is described as forgiveness. That is, the way in which Satan has been defeated and we have been freed, is by God forgiving us (Colossians 1:13–14), and becoming our Lord himself.

Release from adverse verdict of the law

Second, we have been set free from the law – not in the sense that we have no law, for we are under the law of Christ – but in the sense that we have been released from the condemning power of sin, which is the adverse verdict of the law. The Jews were under law in the sense that they knew this condemning verdict all too well. But we Gentiles were also under the law, in the sense that it was by the law that we were excluded from the people of God, alienated from God's promises and without God and without hope in the world. Now, because of the death of Jesus, the power of the law to divide people, and the power of the law to condemn people has been destroyed, *He forgave us all our sins, having cancelled the written code with its regulations, that was against to us, and that stood opposed to us; he took it away, nailing it to the cross* (Colossians 2:13 – 14). Now, through the death of Jesus Christ, both Jew and Gentile together in one body, have access to God on exactly the same terms, by grace (Ephesians 2:11 – 22).

Release from condemnation of judgement

Third, we have been set free from condemnation in the judgement. The Bible says that we have been justified: the judicial verdict of God over our sinful lives has been delivered and he has done the ungodlike thing of *justifying the ungodly*; we already stand acquitted from the verdict of God's judgement, without any works to commend us to God. The result is that we have been reconciled to God: owing to our deep and persistent sinfulness, we were the enemies of God. Now, through what Christ has done by dying for us, we have peace with God, the pacification of our spiritual enemies, the end of enmity, reconciliation. Even more than that, we have now entered into a new covenant with the Lord, sealed with his blood; a covenant relationship which brings forgiveness through his death.

The adopted children of God

Fourth, we have become the adopted children of God. He has purchased us out of misery and darkness, not because we have commended ourselves to him by our righteousness, but sheerly from his grace. On these grounds, the New Testament is able to give us the immense privilege of assurance of God's love. If it depended at all on us, there could be no assurance. But, as Paul says in Romans 5:5, love is poured into our hearts by the Holy Spirit. He is speaking not of our love for God, but of the way in which through the Holy Spirit, God persuades us of his love for us.

The text of Romans 5:1–11 shows us the grounds of this assurance. It is not because of good works which we have done and which may give us a brief and vainglorious boast in the presence of the Lord. Our peace with God comes because we have been justified by faith. Our assurance, our hope, persists despite the suffering which we may pass through. It persists, this utter persuasion that God loves us, because of the great objective fact of the gospel: *at just the right time, when we were still powerless, Christ died for the ungodly ... But God demonstrates his own love for us in this: While we were still sinners, Christ died for us* (Romans 5:6–8).

New creation in Christ

Fifth, we have become a new creation in Christ. You cannot acquire a master like Jesus Christ without transformation of your life. We are not transformed in order to be his; we are transformed as a result of being his. It transforms our attitude to the world. We may have been afraid of evil spirits, fearful of luck or chance, dubious about the future. But the Bible tells us that there is one God in charge of all things and the death of Jesus assures us of his special love towards us, and that we can never be separated from him. The defeat of evil spirits is the victory of the cross in securing our forgiveness, our justification and our adoption. In this way, we who were slaves *to those who were by nature are not gods* (Galatians 4:8), are now secure in the freedom of serving Christ as Lord.

Furthermore, because there is no longer any struggle to make God love us, or to prove worthy of God's love, we are set free to do the things which please him for the right reason. The faith that justifies, the repentant faith which puts us under the Lordship of Christ, is filled with the love of Jesus. We now love him, for he first loved us. Out of this faith and shaped by this love comes obedience, and flowering of the good works which God has prepared for us to walk in. In particular, impelled by the love of Christ for us we find ourselves loving those whom the Lord has united with us in the church, because he has loved the church and has given himself for her. That was always his great intention: to save a particular people. He has not failed.

The life of the Christian is a cross-shaped life. Indeed, as Christians we can never graduate beyond the cross; our piety is cross-centred, or it is hardly Christian. As the master has walked, so do the slaves. He said: *whoever wants to be the first, must be slave of all. For even the Son of Man did not come to be served, but to serve and to give his life as a ransom for many* (Mark 10:44–45). We see in his love two matchless qualities which we are impelled (nonetheless) to imitate: First, a total self-giving, in which no price is too high to pay for the good of the other. Second, a self-giving for those who are our enemies, who have nothing to commend them, who have no merits.

The how and why of redemption

These are five blessings which come from the purchase of broken-down and miserable slaves by Jesus Christ, and their being united to him. I have talked mainly about the *what* of the redemption – that which has flowed from it: reconciliation, forgiveness, victory, transformation. But, *how* is it that the God of justice may achieve these things and still be true to his own character? Here we must turn to the language of atonement.

Some people become very nervous at this question. They believe that there is a danger that we may be too precise. They think that we can know little or nothing about how God has been righteous and saved people at the same time. They would prefer to leave the question of *how* in the sphere of theory and speculation if it is to be handled at all. About such people James Denney said: 'they profess to believe in the fact of the atonement, but they despair of finding any theory of it. There are even some who glory in this situation; it is not with despair, but with triumph, that they find in the very heart of the gospel a mystery which is simply insoluble, in the very focus of revelation a spot of pure impenetrable black.'[1]

Denney is right; our hesitation to be clear robs us of something important. I want to say that we may go as far as the Bible itself takes us. When we do, we have the joy and satisfaction of learning from the Lord himself something of *how it is* that the death of his Son has brought forgiveness and redemption; we cannot understand it all, but what he gives us illumines all the rest, and gives us a proper and an amazing and a joyous sense of satisfaction that he is both just, and at the same time the one who justifies the ungodly who have faith in Jesus (Romans 3:26). At the heart of the universe there is a just God – thank God for that!

They Crucified the Lord of Glory

First of all, let us remember who Jesus is. Paul says that the rulers of this age *crucified the Lord of glory*; they put God to death. We know that the one they crucified was the man Jesus Christ; but we know too that he was both God and man; that in his coming and in his life and in his death we do not see the falling apart of God, but the work of God, the Father and the Son and the Holy Spirit. The Lord who has saved us is the Prince of Peace, mighty to save. It is God himself who has taken this action. He has identified himself with us so absolutely that we see in him the revelation that God understands our sin-induced griefs from within: *a man of sorrows, and familiar with suffering ... he took up our infirmities and carried our sorrows* (Isaiah 53:3, 4) – even in the garbage dumps of Brazil.

The Sacrifice of Jesus

Then let us note that to describe what he has done, the Scriptures use the category of sacrifice. The old sacrifices of bulls and goats could not take away sin, though they point with utmost clarity for the need that we have that our sins should be removed through blood-shedding. But now, *Just as man is destined to die once, and after that face judgement, so Christ was sacrificed once to take away the sins of many people* (Hebrews 9:27). This was a sacrifice of himself; he made it by his choice; so great and all sufficient was it that it has never and can never be repeated, not even sacramentally; we cannot add to it or supplement it. Three great words help us to understand the significance of it.

Substitution

In the first place it was as a *substitute* that he made it; he took the place of those whom he came to save. Certainly he acted on our behalf, as our representative in regard to sin; but his acting on our behalf is precisely because we are powerless to do it ourselves. In that case, to act on our behalf is to act as our substitute, to act in our place: *Very rarely will anyone die for a righteous man*, says Paul, *... while we were still sinners, Christ died for us.* To die for another person must be to die in the place of that person; it is the only way my death for him or her can make sense. In our case, since the wages of sin is death, and since we are sinners, and since Christ has rescued us, it must in some way be by the exchanging of his death for ours: *one died for all, and therefore all died ...* (2 Corinthians 5:14).

Punishment

Secondly it was a *punishment* which he endured by becoming this substitute for us. This of course, was prefigured in Isaiah 53: *he was pierced for our transgressions, he was crushed for our iniquities; the punishment that brought us peace was upon him, and by his wounds we are healed.* The New Testament again and again connects the death of Christ to our sins. This is its great theme. And when it does, it means that God himself is one who actively punishes; it is not merely a matter of sin being its own reward. Thus the New Testament speaks of Christ 'bearing sin', of him 'becoming a curse', even of him 'becoming sin'. There is no doubt as to the significance of these expressions: you 'bear sin' by taking the penalty of sin, by paying the price of sin, by being punished for sin, by receiving in yourself the judgement on sin. *He himself bore our sins in his body on the tree ... by his wounds you have been healed* (1 Peter 2:24). It is useless hoping that there is no such thing as punishment in a just universe. It is useless hoping that *you* will not merit punishment in a just universe. You can only hope that somehow, someone will lovingly bear your punishment *and* that the universe will still be just.

When Christ was handed over by his own people to the pagan occupying power, it was understood to be a mark of judgement. He fell under the curse of God, for when Israel went into exile, that is precisely what was happening. As the story unfolds, say in the Gospel of Mark, there is every sign of the wrath of God being experienced: the betrayal, the abandonment of friends, the twofold negative judicial verdict by those who were the agents of God in justice, the darkness at noonday, the great cry of dereliction from the cross. It is important to see here not some heavenly Trinitarian transaction occurring out of our sight, but the actual, real, in the body acceptance of judgement, by a totally righteous man, for the sake of those who *did* deserve to be forsaken by God. 'In my place condemned he stood.'

Propitiation

Thirdly, there is the word *propitiation*, a word which takes us back to Christ's death as a sacrifice. 'Propitiation' is a personal word: it means to turn aside anger or wrath. I expiate a sin; I propitiate a person. The Scriptures speak of the wrath of God, his holy anger against sin and those who sin against him. His anger is just and thoroughly righteous; it is deserved by us. If there were no anger of God in this universe we would be living in an unjust and hopeless world. But the fact that we are the enemies of God means that we are by nature the children of wrath. It is this which John means when he writes: *He is the atoning sacrifice for our sins, and not only for ours but also for the sins of the whole world* (1 John 2:2).

There is sometimes resistance to this way of talking about the death of Jesus. Such resistance is understandable if it is presented as it were as the loving Son being punished by the angry Father. But such is not the New Testament description. To quote Professor Thiselton, 'Propitiation leads to disastrous distortion, only if we fail to emphasize, that God himself is the *source* of the action, not that Christ 'propitiates' an angry and reluctant God.'[2] It was the Lord of Glory who was crucified for us; unlike the pagan gods, he provided the propitiation himself, of himself. In the great words of James Denney, some say, 'God is love ... and *therefore* he dispenses with propitiation; God is love, say the apostles, for he provides propitiation.'[3]

Likewise people are sometimes troubled by penal substitution, asking how one person can be punished in place of another. Once again the answer is to be found in the Person of the substitute, for in God's way of ordering his universe, the actions of one can be made for another, as in the case of Adam; so, too, by his willing choice, the Lord of glory himself may sustain the cost to be paid by his own penalty, when he saves his own people, unites them with himself and exchanges his righteousness for their sin: *God made him who had no sin to be sin for us, so that in him we might become the righteousness of God* (2 Corinthians 5:21).

However, I believe that the difficulties with the doctrine I have set forth here arise from another source than those I have mentioned. The New Testament makes the connection between our sin and the death of Christ so frequent and so clear, that when the New Testament doctrine of the death of Christ is doubted, it is almost always because of a failure to perceive the seriousness of sin. We falter at accepting the sheer depth of sin, and its enslaving hold on the human heart; we falter at accepting the judgement of sin, the righteousness of that judgement and the seriousness with which the Lord regards iniquity. When Christians make less of sin and judgement than the Bible does, you may be sure that it will show itself first in the doctrine of the atonement and then in the doctrine of justification by faith.

The evangelical theology to which we adhere as members of the Church of England, is of a piece: it is a coherent whole. When we give up, modify, or distort one section, it has unforseen consequences on the whole. I believe that we have been too little aware of this important point and too willing to trade away parts of our theological heritage. The doctrine of penal substitution is inherent to evangelical religion; it is part of the logic of it. That is why in days gone by evangelicals have been in the forefront of the fight to preserve it.

And that is why it is at the very centre of evangelical piety. Twice when Paul talked about the love of Christ he used a very significant past tense. We would say that Christ loves us; he said Christ loved us. He could not graduate beyond the cross of Jesus as the source and power of his religion; as the place at which he gained assurance; as the demonstration beyond any other need of proof, of the grace and love of God. The biblical doctrine of the atonement is a continual reminder of just where we stand with God; it puts us in exactly the right place with regard to him: as helpless sinners, saved ever and only by his grace; always in debt to him; always, only, able to boast because of him; the consideration of the cross fills us more and more with the knowledge of the length and height and depth and breadth of the love of God for us, and it makes us love the Lord more and more.

> In my place, condemned he stood:
> Sealed my pardon with his blood:
> Alleluia!

Notes

1. James Denney, *Studies in Theology* (London: Hodder and Stoughton, 1906) p.106.
2. Anthony Thiselton, *The First Epistle to the Corinthians*, (Carlisle: Paternoster, 2000) p.1191.
3. *idem.*

Chapter 8

The Cross – Power and Weakness

Anthony Thiselton

In the First Epistle to the Corinthians Paul writes,

For the proclamation of the CROSS is folly to those who are on their way to ruin, but the POWER of God to us who are on the way to salvation ... We proclaim a CRUCIFIED Christ: to the Jews an affront; to Gentiles, folly; but to those who are the called (both Jews and Gentiles) a Christ who is God's POWER and God's wisdom. For God's 'foolishness' is wiser than human wisdom, and God's 'WEAKNESS' is stronger than human strength.[1]

It is not surprising that the Jewish and Gentile worlds of Paul's day perceived the very notion of a Christ crucified upon a cross as an affront, as folly, as weakness. Death by crucifixion upon a cross was the most shameful, the most ignoble, and the most disgusting of all possible ways to die. The very notion that a 'Christ' (the Greek translation of the word 'Messiah', meaning 'one anointed by God to do God's work') should end his life in crucifixion could be nothing but folly and an ineffective gesture of weakness: a contradiction in terms; an affront to common sense. It outraged Jewish hopes and Gentile respect for rational understanding.

Jews and Gentiles alike would expect that any divine agent sent by God would be imbued with divine power to overcome all opposition, if need be by force. But Jesus made himself subservient to a

Roman governor, and died a death reserved only for slaves, for terrorists, and by those with no status in society – a death so humiliating, so brutally agonizing, so abhorrent, so disgusting to good taste, that by common consent the cross was never mentioned in civilised society except if necessary on rare occasions by euphemisms which avoided bringing the revolting process of crucifixion before people's minds. As Jürgen Moltmann observes, by elevating the cross into a silver icon, we obscure its ugliness and repulsive horror, by 'surrounding it with roses.'[2]

It is easy to see why Jews and Gentiles who had not yet become Christians regarded the very notion of preaching the cross as folly, as a contradiction, as preaching ineffective weakness. But Paul's more specific point in these verses is that *even Christians* at Corinth have moved the cross from the centre of the stage. They had tried to construct in its place a religion that offered a pathway to public recognition, honour, self-fulfilment, and a high status for the self; and this had little to do with the cross or the gospel. It owed more to their cultural background before they became Christians, on which we shall say more in due course.

Paul consistently keeps the cross at the centre of the stage. He defines the very gospel itself as *the proclamation of the cross* in 1:18. Two or three years before he wrote 1 Corinthians he wrote in Galatians 6:14: *May I never boast of anything except the cross of our Lord Jesus Christ, by which the world has been 'crucified' to me.* In Galatians 3:1 he says that he *placards* (Greek, *prographō*, places on a bulletin board in the public square or city centre) the *CRUCIFIED* Christ. Three or four years after he wrote 1 Corinthians, he declares in Romans, *for I am not ashamed of the gospel*: *it is the power of God for salvation to all who believe,*[3] where once again *the gospel* means the proclamation of the cross.

What can account for these different and irreconcilable views of the cross? Is it power or weakness? It is easy to understand how one person may be repelled by what another perceives as life giving. In the fourth century Chrysostom used two analogies to explain these different apprehensions of the cross. If we become sick or ill, he commented, healthy food may actually repel us, and when we are well again we may long for it. Young children may dislike or even hate what is good for them; but in maturity they will welcome what is for their good. This applies to Paul and Corinth.

Christians at Corinth see the cross as weakness: it encourages feeble dependence, and discourages self-reliance and self-promotion. In the nineteenth century the anti-Christian, anti-theist philosopher Friedrich Nietzsche poured scorn on what he saw as the slavish 'mediocrity' of over-dependent Christians who followed the example of the humility of Jesus. Paul sees the cross as power: the power of God's freely-given gift, to give release from sin, and the start of a new life, freed from the past.

Christians at Corinth see the cross as weakness: for it has none of the rhetorical power of the professional rhetoricians at Corinth, perceived as Paul's rivals. Paul sees the cross as power: power of redemption from bondage, and life under a new Lord.

Christians at Corinth see the cross as weakness: it fails to build on their existing achievements and even sets these aside as irrelevant. Paul sees the cross as power: power to enter a new world, freed from blindness and illusion.

This suggests three headings for the remainder of our reflections. First, **the cross as power to begin a new life**, as Christ through his cross frees us from past penalties and burdens, and gives us new status. Second, the **cross as power to serve a new Lord**, as Christ through his cross frees us from other competing powers, and makes us his own. Third, **the cross as power to enter a new world**, as Christ through his cross frees us from blindness and illusion, and gives us new vision.

1. The Cross as Power to Begin a New Life, as Christ through His Cross Frees Us from past Penalties and Burdens, and Gives Us New Status

Misunderstandings of the power of the cross arose at Corinth because many focused on what they ACHIEVED rather than on what they RECEIVED: the power of God's FREELY GIVEN GIFT. In chapter 4 verse 7 Paul diagnoses the Corinthian problem as their obsession with status, self-promotion, and achievement, exclaiming, *Who sees anything different in you? What do you have that you did not receive? But if you 'received' it, why do you boast as if you did not receive it?*

The power of the cross operates as sheer, unmerited, gift. In this sense perhaps the simplest exposition of the meaning of the cross is that 'Christ did for me *what I cannot do (and could never have done) for myself. He died for me'*. This means, in turn, that the power of the cross is experienced when God takes the initiative, and determines the cross as the place of meeting and of reconciliation with Him. Dietrich Bonhoeffer expresses this brilliantly: 'If it is I who say where God will be, I will always find there a 'God' who in some way corresponds to me, is agreeable to me, fits in with my nature. But if it is God who says whether He will be ... that place is the cross of Christ.'[4] This lies at the very heart of any genuinely evangelical exposition of the cross, and it is also where Paul's theology of the power of the cross conflicts most sharply with misunderstandings at Corinth.

For evangelical Christians this is distinctively bound up with the central belief that 'Christ died in my place', and that God's wonderful 'love without strings' set in all in motion. Even the most conservative of evangelical theologians, Leon Morris, warns us that 'sometimes ... evangelicals have unwittingly introduced division into the Godhead'. Christ did not appease a reluctant Father, for *God was in Christ, reconciling the world to Himself* (2 Corinthians 5:19).[5] The free, sovereign, grace of God is the source and root of the cross, not its fruit. Evangelicals, further, do not limit the meaning of the atonement to this alone, for the New Testament uses a variety of imagery to expound the meaning of the atonement. Nevertheless what characterises our identity *as evangelicals*, alongside our view of Scripture, is our insistence that this forms an irreducible core in the proclamation of the cross.

The logic is irrefutable, provided that we leave room for other dimensions. Professor J. K. S. Reid expressed this well. Two distinct principles operate. On one side Christ wins for us gifts and blessings of which he himself had no need: forgiveness of sins, reconciliation with God, being put right with God. 'Christ wins these benefits for us who himself had no need of them'. But on the other side there is also 'a rule of correspondence': 'Because he lives, we shall live also'; *He who raised Christ from the dead will also give life to your mortal bodies* (Romans 8:11).[6] The very earliest Christian creeds and acclamations (from before Paul's letters) include such doctrinal summaries as *Christ was handed over for our sins and was raised for our justification* (Romans 4:24, 25); and *Christ died for our sins in accordance the Scriptures* (1 Corinthians 15:3).

Our critics often ask, 'Where does *Jesus* say all this?' Strikingly, as Bonhoeffer also points out, Jesus says it at the very point at which many liberal thinkers perceive the heart of a liberal gospel to lie. Jesus exclaims: 'Blessed are the poor! Blessed are the mourners! Blessed are the meek!' and amazingly 'Blessed are those who are persecuted for doing right'. Why? How can it be blessed, happy, or lucky, to be one of these? It is blessed because all of these know *their need*: their agenda is *not how to achieve* but *how to receive*. Hence Jesus does not say, 'Blessed are the powerful', or 'Blessed are the achievers'; but *Blessed are the persecuted, for they shall be called children of God* (Matthew 5:3 – 5, 9 and the parallel in Luke 6:20 – 21).

Jürgen Moltmann brings home to us something of the distinctive suffering of Jesus that *in its fullest sense* can only be *'in my place'*. When Jesus cries, *My God, my God, why have you forsaken me?* he encounters 'God's silence, the hiding of God's face, the eclipse of God, the death of God, hell … abyss … Jesus died the death of God's Son in God-forsakenness.'[7] To be sure, there is also a secondary sense of *participation* in the cross. Paul writes that he experienced a coming to the end of his own strength and what he could bear, to pass on to a resurrection experience. But Christ alone experienced such hell in all its raw depths 'in my place'. We have been delivered from true hell by the power of the cross.

What does this 'power of the cross', then, signify for the Christians of Corinth and for us? It means power to begin a new life, because Christ has freed us from the burden of guilt and shame of past sins and past self-centredness. This is what Paul means when he says in Galatians that he glories in the cross of Christ by whom *the world is crucified to me and I to the world* (6:14). He lets anxious care about himself go: care about his sin and failures; but by the same token he leaves in God's hands as a matter of indifference whether his supposed achievements are really achievements or not. Thus he writes to the Christians at Corinth: *I do not even judge myself; it is the Lord that judges me* (1 Corinthians 4:4).

We have been released, or to use the biblical and Pauline word, 'redeemed'. Paul tells the Christians at Corinth: *You have been bought with a price* (6:20). The word 'redemption' first came into its own when Israel was redeemed from Egypt. The redeemed could leave behind forever their old life of bondage and fear, to begin a new life, with a new identity and a new status, as God's liberated people. But liberation more than redemption is not only redemption *from* the past; not even only redemption by a costly act*; it is also redemption to a new kind of existence*. This is a second aspect of the power of the cross.

2. The Cross as Power to Serve a New Lord, as Christ through His Cross Frees Us from Other Competing Powers

Evangelicals have been criticised for seeing the power of the cross only in terms of freedom from the sins and burdens of the past, and for too often failing to perceive the power of the cross in the present and for the future. We may reply that sanctification *in the present* is the work of the Holy Spirit rather than a direct effect of the cross. But it is *both*. We receive the Spirit through Christ (Romans 8:9), as Lord (1 Corinthians 12:3). Christians at Corinth had forgotten that the gifts of the Holy Spirit remain cruciform. Hence Paul's first exposition on the Holy Spirit and being 'spiritual' concludes: 'But we have the mind of *Christ*' (2:16).

Here the logic is not only that of substitution, ('Christ died for me') but also that of participation ('I am crucified with Christ'). By *sharing in* Christ's death, we shall be raised with him (Romans 6 and 8:11).

Paul reminds those at Corinth that they no longer belong to themselves. He writes, *You have been bought with a price; therefore glorify God in your whole being* (6:20). This sums up the first six chapters: we are temples of the Holy Spirit, purchased by Christ's blood from slavery. Until some ten years ago, many explained this on the analogy of pagan deities' 'purchasing' slaves from Roman or Greek masters to be set free. There are inscriptions from Delphi and elsewhere depicting Athene, Asklepios and other Greek deities redeeming slaves to enjoy freedom. But, as fresh research corroborates, Paul has a different picture, namely that of a purchase that effects a change of owner to a new Lord.[8]

This relates to the cross in three ways. First, in the first century a slave's condition depended on the character of the master or Lord, and for what work or purpose he had purchased them. This could range from menial, punishing toil, to that of a manager over the Lord's business, farm, or accounts. Many did exploit slaves as mere personal property; but some were caring masters, who accorded them trust. We could not explain why some who were in difficulties chose to sell themselves into slavery voluntarily unless at least some situations were tolerable. Slavery could be unspeakably dreadful, or it could be very different.

Paul understands the purchase of the Christian as liberating, but only in terms of belonging to Jesus as Lord. He writes, *If we live, we live to the Lord; if we die, we die to the Lord. Whether we live or die, therefore, we are the Lord's* (Romans 14:7). This is an exultant declaration of trust and obedience to the Lord who has taken over the care of us from ourselves to his own wiser, love.

Second, prior to our redemption, we ourselves carried the burden of caring for ourselves. But after our purchase, who has the care of us now? If we do not over-press a merely partial parallel, we may compare the very best possible feudal Lord as he might care for you as his serf: if you died, he would provide for your widow; if you became injured, he would see that you were nursed to health; if you were in need, he would provide. You are his responsibility.

Thus the Lord gives provision to his purchased people for their every need. He provides *protection*. Those of ill intent would think twice before interfering with the slave of a powerful Lord. Thus, similarly, Christ has redeemed us from hostile powers, whether we think of these as non-earthly forces, or more probably in Paul's view, forces of structural, organized, or corporate evil, beyond merely individual hostility. Christians carry the protective mark of Christ's ownership: the seal of the Holy Spirit. They *belong* to their Lord. He provides *correction*. He does not abandon us to make fools of ourselves or to harm ourselves. Christ is our Wisdom (1:31). He provides *direction*. He is Lord. We belong to him.

3. The Cross as Power to Enter a New World, as Christ Frees Us from Blindness and Illusion, and Gives Us a New Vision

The cross opens up a new world of *reality*. It shatters illusion, just as when we open the curtains, the morning sunshine streams in and disperses the tatters of an idle dream into fading memories of a scrambled, far-fetched, caricature of the world.

One central theme of this Congress has been that evangelicals believe not only in the centrality of the cross, but also in the authority of God's self-revelation in Christ and in Scripture. Revelation means, 'unveiling', like opening curtains to let in the light. Everything looks different in the light of the cross. What we may have perceived as God's 'weakness' becomes manifest as God's power. What we might have perceived as 'folly', we now see as God's wisdom. We see with new eyes. For the cross discloses the very heart of God.

Now, the *very notion of 'POWER'* takes on a new meaning. Under the legacy of Sir Isaac Newton and eighteenth-century rationalism we have tended to construe power in terms of the machine age. Powerful machines are those that apply the maximum force. After Einstein we may perceive power as energy derived from matter and velocity, but at a popular level, we may still think of power as high-voltage electric current, and power in the Christian sphere too readily as 'high voltage religious experience'. We may be influenced by politics and the social sciences, and think of power in terms of majority votes or shallow but forceful, manipulative rhetoric.

Paul insists that the cross undermines such notions of power.[9] The Corinthians were dazzled by what was supposedly impressive and forceful, achieved social ends, and what promoted self-esteem. The notion of Christianity without the cross came dangerously near to the diagnosis of religion put forward by Friedrich Nietzsche: 'the salvation of the soul? – in other words, the world revolves round me!'[10]

Is this view of power peculiar to Paul? Jesus firmly teaches this also. In the beatitudes, as we have seen, Jesus exclaims, not 'blessed are the powerful'; but *Blessed are the meek, the mourners, the persecuted*. Second, in the messianic temptations, Jesus rejected a messiahship based on force, or on an appeal to miracle. He accepted the path of constraint and suffering that led to the cross. Third, in his final entry to Jerusalem he chose the humble donkey rather than the warhorse of worldly power. Finally Jesus declares, *Unless a grain of wheat falls into the earth and dies, it remains just a single grain; but if it dies, it bears much fruit* (John 12:24).

Biological sciences help us to understand that Jesus appeals to a fundamental axiom in God's universe. If an organism is defensive and puts up walls for self-protection, what will survive is only the organism itself, with all its limitations. If an organism yields its life and empties itself, there will emerge some transformed life, for which it has yielded its own.[11] *Whoever gains his life shall lose it, and whoever loses his life shall find it* is built into the very structure of God's creation.

Paul's understanding of power remains a thousand miles away from misunderstandings of 'power' at Corinth. Christians at Corinth drew from the culture around them notions of power as force, influence, and ability to control others sometimes even by manipulative rhetoric. Hence Paul rejects the demand that he should turn rhetorician and convey the gospel *with high sounding cleverness* (2:1–5). He does not want *to know anything except Christ, and a Christ crucified*. Yet why is this problem so acute at Corinth?

Corinth was a bustling, thrusting, busy, commercial city. It boasted two harbours, one to the East and one to the West; it controlled the land route between North and South; it stood at a key crossroads for trade and business. When Julius Caesar re-founded it in 44 BC, Roman soldiers, freed persons, slaves and entrepreneurs flocked there to better their position and status. The Isthmian Games guaranteed a huge income from tourism, and generated a vast demand for goods and services. Springs guaranteed a massive water supply for all needs. Paul's Corinth was a self-sufficient culture, obsessed with the desire for self-promotion; a culture that deified 'power' and 'success'. It assessed truth by what would win approval among market consumers[12] Plutarch writes contemptuously of those who, having failed to rise by their own ability, try to get to the top by fastening onto influential or wealthy patrons like ivy climbing up a tree.[13]

How could Corinth understand the utterly different 'power' that belonged to the cross, or to the grain of wheat that fell into the ground without concern for self-preservation? How could they see Jesus hanging upon the cross of shame and disgrace, as 'God's glorious power'? Only *the cross itself* could bring about such transformation, by drawing them into its world.

Only thus could they hear Paul's proclamation of the cross as one of *power* (1:18, 24; 2:1 – 5). Only thus could transformation occur over making church leaders divisive (1:12 – 17, 3:5 – 4:21); immorality (ch. 5); using law-courts to manipulate fellow-Christians (ch. 6); eating food from pagan temples without concern for the vulnerable (ch. 8 – 10); retaining Roman dining customs at the Lord's Supper, thereby giving poorer Christians second-class food in a second-class room, both different from more esteemed guests (ch. 11); using freely-given gifts of the Spirit to promote the self, with insensitivity towards others (ch. 2 – 14); overlooking the creative power of God in the resurrection (ch. 15).

Conclusion

How do we compare with Christians in Corinth? Or does this very question lead us into a trap? Augustus Toplady wrote:

> Rock of Ages, cleft for me,
> Let me hide myself in Thee;

> Let the water and the blood,
> From thy riven side which flowed,
> Be of sin the double cure,
> Cleanse me from its guilt and power.
>
> Nothing in my hand I bring,
> Simply to Thy cross I cling;
> Naked come to Thee for dress;
> Helpless, look to Thee for grace;
> Foul I to the fountain fly;
> Wash me, Saviour, or I die.

Yet Isaac Watts captures even more strongly the 'New World' of the cross:

> When I survey the wondrous cross,
> On which the Prince of glory died,
> My richest gain I count but loss,
> And pour contempt on all my pride.

For the proclamation of the CROSS is folly to those are on their way to ruin, but the POWER of God to us who are on the way to salvation ... We proclaim a CRUCIFIED Christ: to the Jews an affront; to Gentiles, folly; but to those who are the called (both Jews and Gentiles) a Christ who is God's POWER and God's wisdom. For God's 'foolishness' is wiser than human wisdom, and God's 'WEAKNESS' is stronger than human strength. (1 Corinthians 1:18, 23–25)

Notes

1. 1 Corinthians 1:18, 23–25.
2. Jürgen Moltmann, *The Crucified God* (English translation London: S.C.M., 1974) pp.34–41.
3. Romans 1:16.
4. Dietrich Bonhoeffer, *Meditating on the Word* (English translation Cambridge, MA: Cowley Publications, 1986) p.45.
5. Leon Morris, *Glory in the Cross* (London: Hodder & Stoughton, 1966) p.46.

6. J. K. S. Reid, *Our Life in Christ* (London: S.C.M., 1963) pp.90–91.

7. Jürgen Moltmann, *The Way of Jesus Christ* (English translation London: S.C.M., 1990) pp.166–67.

8. See for example Dale B. Martin, *Slavery as Salvation*, New Haven: Yale, 1990; in contrast to the influential but now dated work by A. Deissmann, *Light from the Ancient East* (English translation London: Hodder & Stoughton, 1927) for a recent classical study, Thomas Wiedemann, *Slavery* (Oxford: O.U.P., 1994) and *Greek and Roman Slavery* (London: Groom Helm, 1981).

9. On the transformative 'world' of the cross in 1 Corinthians see Alexandra R. Brown, *The Cross and Human Transformation* (Minneapolis: Fortress, 1995) and Anthony C. Thiselton, *The First Epistle to the Corinthians* (Grand Rapids: Eerdmans and Carlisle: Paternoster, 2000); and on the transformation of 'power' in Christian theology, see also the Church of England Doctrine Commission Report, *Being Human* (London: Church House Publishing, 2003) pp.32–54.

10. Friedrich Nietzsche, *Collected Works* (English translation London: Allen & Unwin, 1909–13, volume 16, 'The Antichrist') p.186, aphorism 43.

11. John Polkinghorne, ed., *The Work of Love*: *Creation as Kenosis* (London: S.P.C.K., 2001) esp. pp.43–65, but also throughout.

12. For evidence and further details, see Thiselton, *First Epistle to the Corinthians*, pp.1–29 and 46–52.

13. Plutarch, *Moralia*, 805 E-F.

Chapter 9

Conference Sermon

John 18:1–14

Wallace Benn

*Since this was a sermon rather than a read paper, it had a more infor-
mal feel than the two preceding chapters, but in order to catch the
tone of what was said, the spoken nature has not been edited out.*

George[1] and I decided to wear robes this morning to show you
that we're on the cutting edge of mission! But rather more
seriously, we were just saying together before we came in what a
joy it is as evangelical bishops to be here at this Congress and to
have the privilege of taking part in this great occasion. And what
a feast we've had already as we've thought about the Bible, Cross
and Mission.

I turn again with joy to talk about the Cross of our Lord Jesus
Christ. For we can never talk too often about the Cross of Christ and
I want you to turn with me to John chapter 18. It's interesting in the
gospels isn't it, that the whole focus of the gospel moves towards
the last week in the life of Jesus. In John's Gospel, for example, half
of his gospel is about the last week. Everything moves towards the
Cross as the focal revelation of the character of God and the love of
the Lord Jesus for us. It's interesting that John records back in John
chapter 12 what Jesus said *The hour has come for the Son of Man*

to be glorified and again in chapter 13, *Jesus knew that his hour had come.* The Cross was the hour of the glorification of the Lord Jesus, the revelation of the character and saving purposes of God. And John illuminates the key truths about the Cross for us, as well as telling us the story of what actually happened.

When I was a young Christian and began to read the Scriptures I used to think that the Gospels told us the story of what happened, and the Epistles explained why it happened. But the more I look at the Gospels the more I began to understand that the Gospel writers tell us why Jesus died. They not only tell us the story but they tell it in such a way as to illuminate and to show us why he died. John does that very wonderfully, as we'll see in a moment. John's portrait of the arrest, trial and crucifixion of Jesus, as he writes it he paints a picture.

A few months ago, my wife and I went to Amsterdam and we went to Rembrandt's house. I have to say that I'm not a great fan of portrayals of Jesus or indeed of the crucifixion. I never think that any representation of Jesus somehow is adequate, and yet when I went to Rembrandt's house, up on the first floor is a painting of the crucifixion which he painted in 1616, and in a dark room I was riveted as I saw this painting. For Rembrandt's use of light is as if there is a floodlight in the picture on the central figure. That's how John writes his Gospel. The floodlight is on the Lord Jesus, the central figure, and around the Cross we see the expressions, like those Rembrandt paints, of those who encountered the Son of God and saw his death. John compresses the story for us to let us see the crucial points that he wants us to take hold of, that he wants to make to us. And so as he tells us the story as it actually happened, John leaves out some details. Not that he is unaware of, for example, the trial of Jesus before Caiaphas, but he doesn't cover the appearance before Herod of the Sanhedrin, and he simply mentions appearing before Annas and before Pilate. He compresses the story but as he tells it he does it in such a way to illuminate for us who Jesus is and why he came to die. Now please come and look with me in a little bit more detail at the first 14 verses of John chapter 18.

John sets the scene for us in the garden and it's very interesting that he does that. The NIV rather misses the point when it says that it's an olive grove, for 'Gethsemane' of course means a winepress. It's mentioned in the synoptic Gospels, and it's fair to say that it was an olive grove, but the word that John uses is *a garden.* And I want you to notice, if you look down with me into chapter 19 and verse 41, you will see that again John mentions a garden, and it's almost as if his account of the arrest, the trial and crucifixion of Jesus is bracketed by talk about a garden. That's not surprising for this is the gospel, you'll remember, that begins with the reminder of the new creation that God is bringing into being through the coming of his Son and the death of his Son. *In the beginning was the Word and the Word was with God.* John here again sets the scene in a garden and reminds us by so doing, if we know the Old Testament of the Garden of Eden, that Jesus is about to undo the tragedy of the original fall of human beings, the original rebellion of human beings. It's about to be undone by the grace and mercy of God shown to us in his Son and what he's about to do through his death.

Then John tells that Jesus went over the Kidron Valley. Again, for a Bible student, it's a reminder of the greatest king of the Old Testament, King David, who foreshadowed the coming of the coming messianic King, who because of the betrayal of his son Absalom fled from the city, and 2 Samuel 15:23 talks about him going across the Kidron Valley. As we'll see in a moment, Jesus goes across the Kidron Valley suffering from betrayal, but he pauses to pray and to return to be obedient to his heavenly Father. Not to run away from the challenge of what the Father had called him to do but to return and be obedient to death, even death on the Cross.

Then Jesus knowing all that would happen to him came forward and said to them 'Whom do you seek?' (v. 4). What a key question that is. Back in chapter 12, Greeks have come seeking Jesus, but here is a crowd seeking not to know more about who Jesus is but rather to destroy him. Jesus asks the key question *Whom do you seek?* and John gives us a very clear answer. *They answered, Jesus of Nazareth,* Jesus the Man, Jesus the historical man. Now, there is no doubt that Jesus of Nazareth lived on this earth but is that all that can be said of Jesus of Nazareth? No, says John. Jesus said to them, *I am he*, or literally 'I am', and John doesn't let us miss the point. *When Jesus said to them 'I am', they drew back and fell to the ground* (v. 6), as Jesus revealed in a little way who he was. As he spoke the divine name as the Son of God, he did so with such power and authority that those who heard it fell back! *I am*, not just Jesus of Nazareth but the Son of God, God come in human form.

And John tells us that Jesus knew what would happen to him. Look again at verse 4, *then Jesus knowing all that would happen to him came forward and said to them*, and then look down further with me at verse 32, *this was to fulfil the word that Jesus had spoken to show by what kind of death he was going to die.* Remember of course that John has already told us back in 12:32 Jesus said *I, when I am lifted up from the earth will draw all people to myself,* and John adds, *he said this to show by what kind of death he was going to die.* Jesus knew exactly what lay ahead of him and yet John, as he paints the picture and tells the story here of what happens, shows us that Jesus took the initiative.

Here are soldiers coming in a detachment of soldiers and servants of the High Priest looking for him. He steps forward, and he takes the initiative: *who are you looking for? Is it me you're looking for? Here I am! I am.* He took the initiative and in the light of their falling back as he pronounced the divine name, in fact the arrest could only go forward because of his permission. He was arrested John tells us, because he allowed himself to be, and further more one of the great themes of John's account is the fulfilment of Scripture in what happened on that Good Friday. Look down in chapter 19 and see this just as one illustration – in 19:24, *this was to fulfil the scripture, which says they divided my garments among them and for my clothing they cast lots.* Now look back at 18:9, *this was to fulfil word that he had spoken.* So the formula that the apostle used and that John uses here to talk about the fulfilment of Holy Scripture, he also uses to talk about the fulfilment of the word of Jesus. For all that is taking place is in fulfilment of the word of Scripture, God's promises of old. And in fulfilment of what his Son, the living Word, had actually predicted would take place.

John tells us unmistakably that what is happening is the fulfilment of God's plan, predicted long ago. So how different a picture this is of Jesus from the picture of Jesus in *Jesus Christ Superstar*, which paints a picture of a good man, a great man even, but his death was a tragedy. It was a sad end to an otherwise good life. No, said the Gospels, everything pointed towards in the whole ministry of Jesus, towards the hour of his glorification. He came in order to die and that was the fulfilment of God's purposes planned of old, not some tragic end to an otherwise good life.

And look at verse 10, the incident with Simon Peter. What a lovely character Simon is, but here though he illustrates a very important point. There's a ring of truth about this, for Simon is rather shown up here for his lack of understanding of what is going on. For Jesus is not a king of an earthly kingdom, and as you will read on in these chapters, as Jesus stood before Pilate, that becomes very plain. *My kingdom,* said Jesus in verse 36, *is not of this world* and deserves not to be defended by earthly power and might. Peter needed to understand that Jesus could not have been arrested unless he had willed it to be the case, and unless he had permitted it to be the case. Peter was good-hearted here, wanting to defend Jesus, but misunderstanding what is happening.

And then look at verse 11. Jesus said to Peter, *Put your sword into its sheath. Shall I not drink the cup that the Father has given me?* This phrase 'the cup' is used in the Old Testament in two basic ways. First of all it is used about suffering, for example in Psalm 75:8. And Jesus, when he took the cup given to him by the Father, went to the suffering and agony and dereliction of the Cross. But the phrase 'the cup of' is more often used in the Old Testament to refer to the cup of God's wrath. In Isaiah 51:17, it is the Cup of God's wrath, God's righteous judgement against sin. You see, God's wrath doesn't mean that God gets in a pique of anger like we do when we're upset about something. No, it's the steady, measured, righteous anger of God against all that destroys, against all that seeks to undo God's purposes in his world. And Jesus took the cup of God's wrath and drank it to the full. He took that cup with resignation, for the King of this Kingdom, the Son of God was willing to suffer so for me and for you. He took that cup for the people, says John. In verse 14, it was Caiaphas who advised the Jews that it would be expedient that one man should die for the people. And if the description over the Cross written by Pilate *Jesus of Nazareth, King of the Jews* tells us who Jesus, is this comment of Caiaphas tells us why he died. He died for the people, he died for you and he died for me. He took that for the people. He took that for his people, those who would put their trust in him.

Listen to John Stott – and if you go away with one book only from this Congress, go away with *Why I Am a Christian* by John Stott. Listen to what he writes – 'sin and death are constantly bracketed, even riveted through the pages of the Bible. Normally the sin and the death are ours, we sin and we die but when the apostles are writing about the Cross, they make the amazing statement that Christ died for our sins. That is, the sin was ours but now the death, or alienation from God, which is the penalty for sin, was his. This is what is meant by substitutionary atonement. He took our place, he bore our sin, he paid our debt and died our death. And if we ask how Christ died our death we can only point to those three hours of god-forsaken darkness in which Christ tasted the desolation of hell in our place that we might be spared it'.

He died for me and he died for you. And there is something interesting about this death that is mentioned by John, something further here, down at verses 31 and 32. *The Jews said to Pilate it is not lawful for us to put anyone to death* while they could have stoned Jesus by permission. They could have burnt him, they could have killed him in other ways but they wanted him to die a particular death. They wanted him to be crucified because the Law said in Deuteronomy 21:23, *cursed be everyone who dies on a tree.* And John says this was to fulfil the word that which Jesus had spoken to show by what kind of death he was to die. Jesus took God's righteous anger against sin. Because of the great love of the Trinity, Jesus came and was obedient to death. He took that judgement which was what you and I deserve, he took upon his holy shoulders. In my place condemned he stood, sealed my pardon with his blood. Hallelujah! What a Saviour!

Jesus, God's Son, could have stayed in heaven without blame and yet he came and lived among us and died for us. He took our sin upon his holy shoulders and he died for us. And there is just one other thing I want us to notice from John 18 and it's this – the ultimate irony as John tells the story.

I don't know what your name is, or what it means, or whether like me you have a middle name that I won't tell anybody, no matter how much you offer me – but look what John tells us: the crowd chose Barabbas. That name means the 'Son of the Father' and according to one of the manuscripts of Matthew, in Matthew's account we're told that Barabbas was called Jesus Barabbas. And can't you see what John is saying to us? That the crowd chose the wrong 'Son of the Father' and the one that was crucified was no-one less than the Son of THE father, the Lord of Glory. Both Jewish accusers and Roman judge are actors in a drama scripted by divine planning. Even the actions of his enemies are used to bear witness of the glory of the identity of Jesus Christ in what he is in the process here of accomplishing. My dear friends, there is no substitute for Jesus, there is no-one else like him who has stood in for us. Here is a saviour worth following.

May I end with the familiar quotation from C. T. Studd which I think is so relevant: 'If Jesus Christ be God and died for me, then no sacrifice can be too great for me to make for him.' This is the Saviour that John tells us about, this is the account of the arrest and trial and crucifixion of Jesus, but this is more than that this is the explanation of why Jesus died. As we listen to John's account let us allow a bygone spirit to bring us to the foot of the cross in new worship in new wonder and in new surrender to our Saviour and to him be the Glory.

Amen.

Notes

1. George Cassidy, the Bishop of Southwell, who was leading the service.

Mission

Theme 3

Theme 3: Mission

Chris Wright and Vaughan Roberts

The third Congress theme had an evening dedicated to it, which involved presentations and interviews that cannot be reproduced easily. But two of the main stage papers addressed the issues clearly, and to some extent the tensions between them illustrate a tension in the evangelical movement as a whole. It would be easy to describe them as complementary – Chris Wright acknowledges the primacy of evangelism while giving a holistic biblical view of mission, and Vaughan Roberts acknowledges the breadth of our involvement but will not let us escape for the absolute primacy Scripture gives to evangelism. But that is to be too neat, and these papers reflect a deeper questioning, and possibly substantial disagreement, among evangelicals as to what 'Mission' really means. This subject is unfinished business for us.

The Revd Dr Chris Wright is International Ministry Director of the Langham Partnership

The Revd Vaughan Roberts is Rector of St. Ebbe's Church, Oxford

Chapter 10

Whose World?
Whose Mission?

Chris Wright

Introduction

The most fundamental biblical answer to both questions, of course, is 'God's!' It is God's world and it is God's ultimate mission to redeem it.

However, it seems best to start with God in relation to both questions. For *the earth is the LORD's* (Psalm 24:1), and so this is God's world before ever it is ours. And *salvation belongs to our God* – and therefore so does the mission of bringing it about for the whole creation (Revelation 7:10). It is, then, God's world and God's mission.

Mission is the dynamic process by which God will transform the earth of God's own creation, now spoiled by human sin and the powers of evil, into the new heaven and new earth of God's redeemed creation. God's mission is what fills the gap between spoiled creation and new creation. And *the Cross* is at the centre of that whole historical and cosmic process. For salvation belongs not only to our God who sits on the throne, but also to the Lamb who was slain – that is, the crucified and risen Jesus.

But how do we know these things? From the Bible, of course. So even to answer two such basic questions as 'whose world is it?' and 'whose mission is it?' we are driven back to both God's revelation (the Bible), and God's redemption (the Cross). This is similar to the double emphasis of Moses' challenge to Israel in Deuteronomy 4:32–40. There he stresses Israel's experience of God's revelation (at Sinai), and God's redemption (the exodus), and then tells Israel that they have experienced these things so that they now know who God truly is, and what he expects of them. We must therefore likewise learn constantly to understand and evaluate all Christian mission in relation to both – what God has said and what God has done. It is appropriate therefore to link all three together, as we are doing at NEAC – Bible, Cross and Mission.

So, I want to speak about mission and the Bible, and about mission and the Cross; but I also want to see each of those two relationships 'from both ends' – that is in mutual interaction.

A. Mission and the Bible

1. The biblical roots of mission

Traditionally, if we enquired about the biblical basis for Christian mission, we would be pointed to the familiar words of 'the Great Commission' (e.g. Matt. 28:16–20) and related New Testament texts.

But for **Paul**, the architect and engineer of the earliest Christian mission to the gentiles – the representatives of the non-Jewish nations – the scriptural basis for mission went much further back. And of course, in any case, 'the Great Commission' in its present scriptural form in the text of the canonical Gospels did not yet exist in the early decades of Paul's mission. Paul had to justify, to critics who ranged from anxious to downright hostile, both his mission practice and his mission theology on the basis of the Scriptures we now call the Old Testament. But that was no problem to him, for Paul found throughout those Scriptures a rich and deep theology of the mission of God – for the world and the nations, and Paul built his own mission theology on that foundation. Just a few examples:

- Paul goes back to creation, and he sees the mission of God as bringing the whole of the created order to liberation along with the sons of God (Romans 8:18–27). Thus Paul proclaims the resurrection of the messiah as the first fruits of that new creation, and can affirm that when any person is 'in Christ', new creation is already begun (2 Corinthians 5:17).

- Paul goes back to Abraham – and sees the mission of Israel as the people called into existence as the covenant people of God with the express purpose of being the agent of God blessing all nations (Galatians 3:6–8). So crucial is this foundation block of Paul's theology that he calls it the gospel in advance – that is, the good news that God intends to bless the nations (and always had done, from the very call of Abraham).
- Paul goes back to the prophets – and sees God's purpose for the gathering in of the nations to become part of Israel, and of Israel itself coming to renewed faith and restoration, so that by this means all Israel will be saved (as Torah, prophets and Psalms had all declared) (Romans 9–11).

So for Paul, then, the mission of God through Israel and Israel's Messiah, for the salvation of the nations and the renewal of creation, was the clear message of the whole of the Scriptures. His own personal mission as 'apostle to the nations' was thus grounded in the Bible. For Paul, biblical theology was a theology of mission – the mission of God.

Jesus did the same thing. Not only did he understand his own personal mission in the light of the Scriptures of the Old Testament, he also taught his disciples to see their mission in the same light and on the same foundation.

This is what is written, he taught them, in a lecture on Old Testament hermeneutics delivered on the very day of resurrection, *The Christ will suffer and rise from the dead on the third day, and repentance and forgiveness of sins will be preached in his name to all nations, beginning at Jerusalem. You are witnesses of these things* … (Luke 24:46–48).

Jesus is not quoting any particular verse here (doubtless he did on the road to Emmaus; there are plenty to choose from). Rather he is saying that this is the whole point and thrust of the Old Testament Scriptures as a whole. They lead purposefully to the *double* fulfilment of (a) the death and resurrection of the Messiah, and (b) the preaching of the gospel to all nations. The Old Testament, argues Jesus, leads both to the messiah and to mission – and that is how disciples of Jesus (whose minds have been opened by him to understand it) must read it.

For Jesus then, the Old Testament was as much about mission as it was about himself. Or rather, the two are inseparable parts of the same fundamental reality – the saving mission of God. If you know who Jesus is from the Scriptures (that he is the Messiah of Israel who embodied their identity and their mission); and if you know what Israel is from the Scriptures (that they were called into existence to be a 'light to the nations'); then, to confess Jesus as Messiah is to commit yourself to his mission to the nations. You can't have one without the other – not if you believe the Scriptures and read them as Jesus taught his disciples to.

The necessity of mission is as rooted in the Bible as the identity of the Messiah.

Luke's account here focuses on Jesus as *Messiah*. Matthew's comparable account of the post-resurrection teaching of Jesus records Jesus putting it in terms of his identity and authority as *Lord* – unquestionably echoing the name of Israel's God, Yahweh, the LORD, in the Scriptures. *All authority in heaven and on earth has been given to me. So, as you go, disciple the nations ...* (Matthew 28:18 – 19). The connection is again very clear – the logic of mission depends on the identity of Jesus. Or as John Stott has often expressed it, 'Mission is an inescapable deduction from the universal Lordship of Jesus Christ.'[1]

For both Paul and Jesus, then, the roots of mission as they understood it were deeply biblical – that is, for them of course, deeply Old Testament. For it was in those Old Testament Scriptures that they discerned the saving mission of God, which Jesus embodied and fulfilled, and which Paul devoted his life to proclaiming to the nations.

2. The missional roots of the Bible

It is not enough, however, just to say that mission has a solid biblical foundation, we also need to see that the Bible itself has its roots in mission. That is, the Bible is the product of God's engagement through God's people in God's world for God's ultimate purpose for the nations and the world. The documents which now collectively form our canon of Scripture emerged as God's people (in both testaments) wrestled with the issues thrown up by their identity, role and mission in the context of a fallen world of surrounding nations, cultures and religions. The human contexts within which the divine word was spoken were precisely the contexts of God's own revelatory and redemptive work.

In my chapter, 'Truth with a Mission' in the Congress book, *Fanning the Flame*, I have outlined this point further. There I survey how the Bible presents to us God with a mission (the biblical God is consistently presented as having a purpose, plan or goal towards which he works – both in the creation narrative and in the longer narrative of redemption in history). It also presents humanity with a mission – to rule over the rest of creation (Genesis 1), and to serve and watch (or keep) the earth (Genesis 2). Christians (who are also, one needs to recall, humans), are called to care for the earth because of the one to whom it belongs (the earth is the LORD's), and the one for whom it is destined (Christ, the reconciler and heir of all things). Earthkeeping is part of our service of Christ. And of course the Bible presents Israel with a mission (not in the sense of being 'sent' anywhere, but of being the agent of God's blessing to the nations, a light to the nations). To Israel God gave his law, to share with them his own passion for justice, integrity and compassion, and special concern for the weak, poor and marginalized. So Israel became not merely the bearer of the truth about the living God, but also a paradigm of the way God wants human society to function. Centrally, the Bible presents Jesus with a mission. He certainly claims to have been 'sent', to fulfil God's purpose for Israel, and thereby to fulfil God's saving purpose for humanity and all creation. And finally the Bible portrays the church with a mission – sent by Christ to disciple the nations, to be and to do, to preach and to live, to share and to show, the good news.

So from beginning to end, the Bible is 'missional', by its very existence and by its comprehensive message. Mission then has to be a prime hermeneutical key for our own Bible reading and teaching. Jesus opened the eyes of the disciples, *so that they could understand the scriptures* – not 'so that they would *know* the scriptures' (they knew them better than most of us as well-taught Jews), but so that they would understand what they are all about – namely the mission of the Messiah and of the Messiah's people, old and new.

Conclusion

To conclude this first section, then, and put both our points together:

Our theology and practice of mission must be biblical

That is to say, our mission must be based on the whole message of the whole Bible – including the whole range of the Bible's concerns and teaching. The Bible renders to us the amazing breadth and depth of the creative and redemptive love of God, his total response to our total need. It shows us his loving care for creation, and for all human lostness, need, pain and peril. It shows us the depth of his anger at sin, his justice in history, his engagement in social, political and economic life, his standards for personal integrity and ethics. It shows us his faithfulness, mercy and compassion. It shows us his unwavering purpose ultimately to bless the nations and redeem creation. We need to ensure that our mission is as holistic as God's mission, that our concerns are as wide as God's concerns, that our gospel is as good news as God's is. All this was reiterated in the Limuru Statement of the second International Conference of EFAC (the Evangelical Fellowship in the Anglican Communion – of which CEEC is the English member): 'We re-affirm that biblical mission is intrinsically holistic'. So our mission must be biblical, but also …

Our reading and teaching of the Bible must be missional

Again, it was Jesus who points the way on this. 'This is how you must read your scriptures', he says to his disciples – not merely to prove who Jesus is, but also to understand the necessity of repentance and forgiveness being preached to the nations. Evangelicals have generally been good at reading the Bible in a Messiah-centred way, but not so good at reading it for mission (and certainly not reading the Old Testament for mission, even though it was the Old Testament Scriptures Jesus was referring to).

Yet the whole Bible renders to us those great realities and truths which impel us into mission. This is the God we worship. This is the story we are part of. This is the people of God to whom we belong. This is the goal to which all of history and the whole universe are heading. What then must be the mission of God's people in the light of these massive biblical truths?

I am sometimes amazed and saddened, when preaching at 'Missionary Weekends' or similar events, that members of the congregation even in large evangelical churches noted for their 'Bible ministry', can come up to me afterwards and say they've never heard mission preached in that way from the Bible before (particularly if I've used an Old Testament text). What Bible is it that is being preached then? Surely, to claim to be 'biblical', and yet to fail to teach and be committed to mission, is seriously to miss the plot – both in the metaphorical sense of having missed the whole point of being a Bible-centred community at all, and in the literal sense of missing the plot of the whole biblical grand narrative.

B. Mission and the Cross

1. A mission-centred theology of the Cross

We have seen that the Bible presents to us God's own mission to redeem and renew his whole creation. Every dimension of that mission led inexorably to the Cross of Christ. ***The Cross was the unavoidable cost of God's Mission***

It was the purpose, goal or mission of God:

    1.1 to deal with the guilt of human sin, which had to be punished for God's own justice to be vindicated. – And at the Cross God did so, by taking that guilt and punishment upon himself in the person of his own Son. For *the LORD has laid on him the iniquity of us all* (Isaiah 53:6), and *Christ himself bore our sins in his own body on the tree* (1 Peter 2:24).

1.2 to defeat the powers of evil, and all the forces (angelic, spiritual, directly or by human agency, – 'seen or unseen'), that oppress, crush, invade, and spoil human life. – And at the Cross God did so, having disarmed the powers and authorities ... triumphing over them by the Cross (Colossians 2:15).

1.3 to destroy death, the great invader and enemy of human life in God's world. – And at the Cross God did so, when by Christ's death *he destroyed the one who holds the power of death* – the devil (Hebrews 2:14).

1.4 to remove the barrier of enmity and alienation between Jew and Gentile, and by implication ultimately all forms of enmity and alienation. – And at the Cross God did so, for *he himself is our peace, who has made the two one and has destroyed the barrier ... to create one new humanity out of the two, thus making peace, and in this one body to reconcile both of them to God through the Cross, by which he put to death their hostility* (Ephesians 2:14 – 16).

1.5 to heal and reconcile his whole creation, the cosmic mission of God. – And at the Cross God did so, in anticipation, for it is his ultimate will through Christ *to reconcile all things, whether things in heaven or things on earth, by making peace through his blood shed on the Cross* (Colossians 1:20 – the all things here must clearly mean the whole created cosmos, since that is what has explicitly been created by Christ and for Christ (vv. 15 – 16), and has now been reconciled by Christ (v. 20).

So then, all these huge dimensions of God's redemptive mission are set before us in the Bible. God's mission was that:

- sin should be punished and sinners forgiven
- evil should be defeated and humanity liberated

- death should be destroyed and life and immortality brought to light
- enemies should be reconciled, to one another and to God
- creation itself should be restored and reconciled to its creator

And all of these led to the Cross of Christ. The Cross was the unavoidable cost of God's mission – as Jesus himself accepted, in his agony in Gethsemane: *not my will, but yours, be done.*

Yes, it is so important that we have a sound and biblical doctrine of the atonement. But let us remember, first, that we are not saved by a theory, but by the historic reality that God sent his Son into the world and his Son willingly gave up his life on the Cross in fulfilment of that mission. It was the unfathomable determination of the saving mission of God that led to those six hours on a Friday outside Jerusalem, to that bleeding body stretched on two pieces of wood, to a torn curtain and a quaking earth, to that awful cry of dereliction, *My God, my God, why have you forsaken me?*, and to that triumphant shout of achievement, *It is finished!* For it was indeed on the Cross that Jesus accomplished the mission of God, for *God was in Christ, reconciling the world to himself.*

And let us remember, second, that a full biblical understanding of the atonement (of which the above points are the merest sketch), goes far beyond the matter of personal guilt and individual forgiveness. That Jesus died in my place, bearing the guilt of my sin, as my voluntary substitute, is the most gloriously liberating truth, to which we cling in glad and grateful worship with tears of wonder. That I should long for others to know this truth and be saved and forgiven by casting their sins on him in repentance and faith, is the most energising motive for evangelism. But there is more in the biblical theology of the cross than individual salvation, and there is more to mission than evangelism. The gospel is good news for the whole creation (to whom, according to the longer ending of Mark, it is to be preached, Mark 16:15, cf. Ephesians 3:10). To point out these other dimensions of God's redemptive mission (and therefore of our committed participation in God's mission), is not (as sometimes alleged) 'watering down' the gospel of personal salvation, but rather setting it firmly and affirmatively within its full biblical context of all that God has achieved and will finally complete, through the Cross of Christ.

2. A Cross-centred theology and practice of mission

So, we have seen that the Cross was the unavoidable cost of God's mission. But it is equally true, and biblical, to say that *the Cross is the unavoidable centre of our mission*. This is so in two ways.

2.1 all Christian mission flows from the Cross – as its source, its power, and as that which defines its scope. It is vital that we see the Cross as central to every aspect of holistic, biblical mission – that is, of all we do in the name of the crucified and risen Jesus. It is a mistake, in my view, to think that our evangelism must be centred on the Cross (as of course it has to be), but that our social engagement and other forms of practical mission work, have some other theological foundation or justification. Why is this? Because in all forms of Christian mission in the name of Christ we are confronting the powers of evil and the kingdom of Satan – with all their dismal effects on human life and the wider creation. If we are to proclaim and demonstrate the reality of the reign of God in Christ – that God is king, in a world which likes still to chant 'we have no king but Caesar' and his many successors, including mammon – then we will be in direct conflict with the usurped reign of the evil one, in all its legion manifestations. We will find ourselves engaged, as Sue Hope[2] put it, in 'hand to hand conflict with darkness'. This is the unanimous testimony of those who struggle for justice, for the needs of the poor and oppressed, the sick and the ignorant, as much as those (frequently the same people) who struggle evangelistically to bring people to faith in Christ as Saviour and Lord. In all such work we confront the reality of sin and evil, challenging the darkness of the world with the light and good news of Jesus Christ and the reign of God through him.

By what authority can we do so? With what power are we competent to engage the powers of evil? On what basis can we challenge the chains of Satan, in word and deed? Only the Cross. Only in the Cross is there forgiveness of sin, the defeat of evil powers, release from the fear of death, the reconciling of enemies, the healing of creation.

The fact is that sin and evil constitute bad news in every area of life on this planet. The redemptive work of God through the Cross of Christ is good news for every area of life touched by sin – which means every area of life. Bluntly, we need a holistic gospel because the world is in a holistic mess. And by God's incredible grace we have a gospel big enough for all that sin and evil has touched. And every dimension of that good news is good news utterly and only because of the blood of Christ on the Cross. Ultimately all that will be there in the new and redeemed creation will be there because of the Cross. And conversely, all that will not be there (suffering, tears, sin, corruption, decay and death), will have been destroyed by the Cross.

So it is my passionate conviction that holistic mission must have a holistic theology of the Cross. That includes the conviction that the Cross must be as central to our social engagement as it is to our evangelism. There is no other power, no other resource, no other name, through which we can offer the whole gospel to the whole person in the whole world, than Christ crucified and risen.

2.2 All Christian mission must be shaped by the Cross. If the Cross was the only way for the mission of God, if it was the only way for Jesus Christ himself, then it is likewise the only way for us – us who follow him and share his mission. Discipleship unavoidably commits us to mission. The Cross is an unavoidable dimension of discipleship.

We cannot, of course, 'replicate' the Cross of Christ himself. We do not suffer redemptively or vicariously as Christ did. His Cross was, as we are so beautifully reminded, 'the full, perfect and sufficient sacrifice, oblation and satisfaction for the sins of the whole world' (Book of Common Prayer). Yet, as Paul affirms, there is that about Christian mission and the suffering it necessarily entails that means entering into the fellowship of Christ's suffering. David Zac's chapter in *Fanning the Flame* illustrates this from the Cross-focused suffering of significant (and often unsung) African missionaries.

The way of authentic Christian mission, then, is the way of the Cross, the way of suffering and sacrifice – just as Paul claimed that weakness, suffering, persecution and contempt, far from being the *disqualifications* that the Corinthians thought in their embarrassment at what was happening to their so-called apostle, were paradoxically the authentic marks of a genuine apostle of the crucified Christ.

Mission is cross-shaped or it is a betrayal of the Crucified. God's mission required Jesus to take up his Cross and obey his Father. Our mission requires us to take up our Cross and follow the Son.

Conclusion

We have seen, then, that our understanding of the Bible and the Cross must be shaped by mission – the mission of God.

And we have seen that our theology and practice of mission must be shaped by the Bible and the Cross.

Let our mission, then, be as broad as the Bible and as deep as the Cross, for the glory of the One who gave us both.

Notes

1. From his oral lecture, 'Jesus Is Lord: A Call to Radical Discipleship'.
2. In an earlier address to the Congress.

Chapter 11

Getting the Message Out

Vaughan Roberts

A young student was in despair. Her life was in turmoil and she felt a deep emptiness within. Somehow she knew she needed God, but she had no idea where to find him. One Sunday, on the way to the supermarket, she saw crowds of young people going into a church and she began to wonder if she might find what she was looking for inside. But she did not go in. It was a frightening, unfamiliar place – she wouldn't know where to sit, when to stand or what to say; so she walked away. There are many like her: aware of a spiritual hole in their lives, but feeling completely disconnected from church and not looking there for answers. We must take some of the blame for that: we have too often hidden the precious jewel of the gospel behind heavy ecclesiastical doors.

The student returned the following Sunday, but once again she couldn't bring herself to go in. She was back again on the third week and would have turned away if an elderly saint hadn't spotted her and asked if she wanted to go in. Three months later she came to Christ. But most people will not persevere like that. They won't even get to the door, let alone go in. If current trends continue, attendances in Anglican churches will be down to two-thirds of the current level by 2030, and there will be almost no children.[1] So our theme, 'Getting the Message Out' is vitally important. The Lord Jesus said 'Go', but for too long we have been saying 'Come' – 'Come to our buildings, our activities, our territory' but people are not coming any more. If we want to begin to impact our desperately needy society and draw people to Christ, we will need to open up the doors and go to them. We must commit ourselves to the task the Lord Jesus gave his disciples: to be his witnesses to the ends of the earth and to the end of time. If we are to do that effectively, it will involve courageous, radical action. The gulf between society and the church, and more importantly, society and Christ, is so great that mere tinkering will not be enough. If we are to begin to make an impact there will have to be radical, costly change in us individually, in our churches, and in our denomination. All I can do in this brief talk is to begin to suggest what that might mean in practise by pointing to 'four M's'.

1. Mission

Mission is a very slippery word. It is rather like motherhood and apple pie – everyone believes in it. It appears in every diocesan mission statement or strategy document, but what does it mean? The word is so broad now that it encompasses almost everything. So we can all affirm the centrality of mission and yet mean very different things by it.

It is time we evangelicals reaffirmed the priority of evangelism. Of course it's right that we are concerned for the whole person, the whole of society and the whole created order. God is and so should we be. There are many terrible problems in our world: ecological, political, sociological, and we should do all we can in the name of Christ to alleviate them. But the greatest problem that faces human beings is spiritual. It is our great privilege and responsibility to proclaim the solution to that problem in Christ. Evangelicals are gospel people. We have always had our differences on secondary matters, but we are bound by common convictions. We believe in **sin**: it is universal and very serious, leading us all under the condemnation of a holy God and facing eternity without him. But we also believe in **salvation**: achieved uniquely by the Lord Jesus Christ by his substitutionary death on the cross. All who trust in him are justified and fully reconciled to God. And we believe in the **Spirit**: sent by God to enable sinful human beings to turn to Christ so that they might be born again and have the certain hope of heaven. It is those truths about sin, salvation and the Spirit which led Wesley and Whitfield to travel the length and breadth of the country preaching the gospel. The same conviction spurred many thousands over the last two centuries to go to the ends of the earth at great personal cost. And now the baton has been handed to us in the twenty-first century. We are called to be Christ's missionaries here in Britain in our generation. If we are to begin to do that job effectively we will have to think radically. Our society has changed and, if we are to reach it with the gospel, we must change too.

We are too often stuck in the old patterns in our thinking. We are too focused on our buildings. If people won't come to us, we should go to them: in the schools, offices, hospitals, residential care homes, pubs and fitness centres. In so doing, we must be prepared to go outside, not just our buildings, but our parishes too. The parochial system is a great resource for mission. It means we've got a presence everywhere, and it says that we are committed to the whole nation. But it also has limitations. It focuses on neighbourhood outreach, reaching local people through their local church. That can be very effective in evangelising those for whom the neighbourhood is the main locus of their existence, such as the elderly, children, and parents at home with their children. But what about the very large number of people for whom home is little more than the place where they sleep? They function primarily in networks, not neighbourhoods – groups built around shared interests, ethnicity and professions. We'll need a very different approach to reach them. And what about those other areas in the city, or the villages nearby, where there is little or no gospel outreach, either because the vicar never preaches the gospel or because the church is small and under resourced? Surely we should be concerned for those areas too?

It would be wonderful if we evangelicals were able to unite and work together, not simply in what we oppose, but in what matters most to us – the work of mission. Do we ever meet together to discuss and pray about the unevangelised areas, groups and networks in our locality? Sometimes we will wish to work through the structures of the Church of England. At other times we'll work most effectively with free churches. Our concern is for the name of Christ in our land

and not for any one denomination. A church's ideas for mission may not be welcomed by denominational authorities; radical thinking seldom is. But let's make sure we support any evangelical church when it takes a new initiative in evangelistic mission, rather than joining the chorus of disapproval. Better still, let's dream dreams together and present them unitedly to the Diocesan authorities. That will increase the chance of permission being granted. And sometimes if it is not, we'll need to go ahead anyway. Let's not wait forever for the initiative to come from the top down. The responsibility is with us – the local church is the key agent in mission. We must ensure that we place mission right at the heart of our priorities.

2. Morality

I hope at least a part of you groans at the mention of that word. Perhaps you think, 'Can't we just focus exclusively on mission for a while without having to think about the divisions over morality which are tearing the Anglican communion apart?' But of course those divisions impinge directly on our mission. Those who say that sex outside heterosexual marriage can be moral are gravely damaging the reputation of the church in many parts of the world, not least in places where there is a substantial Muslim population. They are watering down the gospel with its call to repentance and causing great spiritual danger to many.

The events of the last few months have issued a wake-up call to us. We have been used to looking at some of the events in North America and saying to ourselves, 'It couldn't happen here – at least for a long time'. But then came the Reading affair[2] and a number of English bishops spoke quite openly about their support for same-sex unions. Others argued against them simply on pragmatic or ecclesiological grounds. But we believe that even if the church wants to change its mind, the Bible won't change its position. God's mind won't change and we are right to demand a clear theological lead from our archbishops and our bishops, not just a political lead. It has become clear that we are faced, not simply with two points of view, but two religions: one which seeks to submit to Scripture, and the other which feels free to put it on one side. Those two positions are irreconcilable. It is inevitable that they will gradually drift apart and there will be some kind of realignment in world Anglicanism. Sooner or later, that is bound to have significant structural implications for the Church of England, and that in turn, will have a huge effect on mission for good or ill.

We saw a remarkable degree of evangelical unity during the Reading controversy, but I am nervous that we will now return to where we were before. It seems unlikely that there will be many more clear-cut occasions when we'll all agree to make a stand together. Instead of standing unitedly against false teaching, there is a great danger that we will tear ourselves apart by rowing over our different responses to what's going on. That will make it much easier for a divide and rule policy to work against us and we could lose the battle. Some will get so used to saying 'No – this isn't the moment to take action' that their 'Not nows' become 'Never' and they lose the nerve to make a stand at all. Others will take decisive action. But they'll do it unilaterally and will give the impression that those who don't do exactly what they're doing are unprincipled. There will just be a small number of them who will easily be picked off. Their property will be confiscated and they will be pushed into the margins and then they'll form some tiny 'Church of England Continuing' grouping that has no real impact on the nation.

But it needn't be like that – it mustn't be! Let's determine to be absolutely united on the principles. We are mainstream Anglicans standing with the Scriptures, the formularies, the Creeds, and with the vast majority of our Anglican brothers and sisters throughout the world. And when any bishop, diocese, or province endorses what is morally wrong, they're taking themselves outside the bounds of Anglicanism. We must continue to affirm that with bold clarity. No doubt, as we do so, we'll differ on policy. It's unrealistic to expect that we'll all agree on a common response to what is happening. But when we take different action at different times, let's do all we can to support one another. We might not do what that church down the road has done. But if they've done it out a concern for the truth of Scripture and the name of Christ, let's make sure we support them to the hilt, as I hope we'll support our beleaguered friends in North America. Let's insist together that they are authentic Anglicans, who must not be pushed out of their buildings, who should be allowed proper orthodox oversight and who must not be sidelined into an ecclesiological backwater.

3. Ministry

Mission is the task of the whole people of God: all Christians are called to be full-time ministers of Christ as we offer our lives in his service. But to be equipped for that task, our churches need to be led by suitably gifted and trained pastors. There is a desperate need for the recruitment, training and deployment of a whole new generation of gospel ministers. We must not think 'How many clergy do we need to look after the church as it is?' the question should rather be 'How many pastors, evangelists and church planters do we need to reach the nation?' The answer is many, many more.

a. Recruitment

This is the responsibility, first and foremost of the local church. We all need to commit ourselves to praying that other Lord's Prayer that Jesus urged his disciples to pray: *Ask the Lord of the harvest to send out labourers into the harvest field* (Matthew 9:38). As we pray, we should be actively looking for such labourers. We should encourage those who are godly and have the right gifts to consider a lifetime of gospel ministry, whether at home or abroad, in the Church of England or elsewhere.

b. Training

Proper training is vitally important. The local church undoubtedly has a central role to play in that. I'm a keen supporter of the apprenticeship model of training.[3] But I still believe the colleges are crucial, especially for those who will spend many years in full-time ministry. They need to have a thorough training in theology, and that takes time. It also costs money, but it's money well spent. If in time, central church funds no longer fully provide the necessary financial support, we must find it in other ways. The future of our colleges is currently under review and, indeed, under threat. We must work together to ensure that they are able to maintain and strengthen their evangelical identity. There is pressure from some quarters to move towards colleges which represent all the traditions of the Church of England rather than being aligned to any one. That would be disastrous. It would hardly be likely to produce clergy with the clear gospel convictions they'll need to be effective evangelists. They are more likely to end up battered and confused.

c. Deployment

Having recruited and trained evangelical ministers, we must be able to deploy them. Once again, let me stress that we are all ministers. We should put great effort into equipping the laity and including them in our leadership teams. But there is also a need for more trained full-timers. We must have the freedom to employ extra workers. If they are ordained, there is surely no good reason for a bishop not to license them. Extra staff cost money, which is always in limited supply. We should be asking tough questions about the best way of financing our mission. The diocesan quota system often has the effect of taxing and limiting growth in some churches, while encouraging an unhelpful dependency culture in others. We must be generous, but we must also be responsible with our money. That may sometimes mean paying less than is demanded by the diocese and re-directing the extra money in the cause of mission, both in our churches and in other churches we support.

4. Meekness

I'm aware that what I've said might have come across as a bit too strident and rather arrogant. We often appear like that to non-evangelicals. We can give the impression that we think the ball is at our feet: 'We've got the numbers, the spiritual vitality and the financial muscle. If we could just adopt the right strategy, then we'd change the Church of England and the whole nation.' But we need to remember the words of Jesus, *The meek will inherit the earth.* Not the strident, not the great strategists, but those who humbly depend on their God.

Iain Murray, in his biography of Martyn Lloyd-Jones, comments: 'His basic unease with English evangelicalism was its failure to see its true spiritual power'.[4] It's a telling comment. I hope very much that NEAC will draw us together – united around the great truths of the Bible and the gospel of Christ crucified. If we could stop squabbling and join together in the cause of evangelism we could be so much more effective. But even if that happens, let's remember how weak and helpless we are. We can't achieve anything. We depend entirely on the Sovereign God having mercy and using us despite our hypocrisy, our factionalism, our pride; having mercy on our denomination, despite its frequent tolerance of error and evil; and having mercy on our nation, despite the corruption that increasingly abounds. So, first and foremost, we need not to look to ourselves, our leaders, organisations and strategies. We need to look to our God. We must come before him in meekness and commit ourselves to urgent prayer, pleading with him to act in this nation for the glory of his Name.

Notes

1. Bob Jackson, *Hope for the Church* (London: Church House Publishing, 2002) p.12.
2. In the summer of 2003 Canon Dr Jeffrey John was nominated as the next Bishop of Reading, a post within Oxford Diocese where Vaughan Roberts is a Rector. Dr John had a long-term same-sex partner, although he insisted the relationship was celibate, and was a leading advocate of the acceptability of gay lifestyles at all levels of the church. His appointment caused an uproar, not least within the Diocese, and he eventually withdrew his acceptance.
3. For more information see www.ninethirtyeight.org
4. Iain Murray, *D. Martyn Lloyd-Jones,* Vol II (Edinburgh: Banner of Truth, 1990) p.163.

Homosexuality

Homosexuality

Gordon Wenham and Edith M. Humphrey

Much to the surprise of the media, it had never been the planning team's intention to hold a Congress on the subject of homosexuality. In fact, the feeling from the outset had been that the Congress was a chance for us to address our agenda rather than being forced to address the issues that others want us to discuss. But as the months leading into the Congress unfurled, and as the Anglican communion entered into increasingly difficult times, it became clear that we could not avoid what was, for many, the headline story of Anglicanism. So it was decided to change the programme late in the day, and include a high level briefing for the constituency, to give an outline of both thinking and pastoral practice. Much of the presentation involved a panel answering questions from the floor, but the two critical papers by Gordon Wenham and Edith Humphrey represent the best current evangelical thought on the subject, driven by biblical, systematic and pastoral concerns.

Professor Gordon J. Wenham is Professor of Old Testament at the University of Gloucester

Professor Edith M. Humphrey is Associate Professor of New Testament at Pittsburgh Theological Seminary

Chapter 12

The Old Testament and Homosexuality

Gordon Wenham

In this short paper I want to make five points.

1. The OT often refers to homosexual activity – always negatively.
2. The Genesis texts used by Jesus to justify his understanding of marriage rule out same-sex intercourse.
3. Leviticus bans every kind of same-sex intercourse, not just homosexual rape or pederasty. These laws were endorsed by the Jerusalem council as binding on all Christians (Acts 15).
4. Both the OT and the NT are reacting to cultures that tolerated homosexual behaviour to a greater or lesser extent. This parallels our situation.
5. There are some significant scholarly discussions of the issues.

1. Passages Condemning Homosexual Acts

Let us begin by listing the passages that explicitly condemn homosexuality. They range from the well-known story of the attempted homosexual rape of the visitors to Sodom in Genesis 19:4–7, sometime in the era of Abraham about 2000 BC, through the condemnations in the law (Leviticus 18:22; 20:13; Deuteronomy 22:17–18), probably the thirteenth century BC, another proposed homosexual rape in Gibeah about 1150 BC (Judges 19:22–23), the references to male prostitutes in the books of Kings (1 Kings 14:24; 15:12; 23:7) tenth to seventh centuries BC, Ezekiel (16:49–50) and Ben Sira's (16:8) reference to the sin of Sodom, in the sixth and second centuries BC. In all these references it is clear that the biblical writers strongly disapprove of the practices mentioned. Nowhere in the Old or New Testaments are homosexual acts approved of.

Leviticus (18:24–30) says that the Canaanites were vomited out of the land because of their sexual immorality. This is foreshadowed in the deeds of their forefather Ham. The odd little story about Noah's drunkenness in Genesis 9:20–27 has puzzled commentators: what is going on? Why should Ham be cursed just for seeing his father's nakedness? Or did he do something more than look? 'Seeing someone's nakedness' is occasionally a euphemism for having sexual intercourse with someone (e.g. Leviticus 20:17). If this is the case here, it would be easier to understand the curse. For in this case Ham could be guilty of three sins at once, homosexual intercourse, incest (sex with his father) and rape (without his father's consent). This was the way that the Canaanites misbehaved according to other texts.

I am not wholly persuaded of this interpretation. It may be that Ham only looked at his naked father with incestuous homosexual intent, (cf. Jesus: *But I say to you that everyone who looks at a woman with lustful intent has already committed adultery with her in his heart* [Matthew 5:28 ESV]). But this makes the same point as the other interpretation even more forcibly. If Ham is cursed, just for looking, how much more serious is actual homosexual intercourse and incest.

2. The Importance of Genesis 1 and 2

So the condemnation of homosexual acts runs from Genesis to the Apocrypha. But this attitude does not begin in Genesis 9 but in Genesis 1 and 2. Modern literary theorists point out that often an author's key ideas are found near the beginning of his work. If you want to understand his premises and underlying assumptions, read the beginning very carefully. Now as Edith has already pointed out Genesis 1 and 2 are quite explicit about the purpose of human sexuality. The creation of mankind is summed up in Genesis 1:27:

> *So God created man in his own image,*
> *in the image of God he created him;*
> *male and female he created them.*

As far as Genesis is concerned, the division of humans into two sexes is as fundamental as the fact that we are all made in God's image. But what is the purpose of making us in two sexes? Genesis gives the obvious answer: *And God blessed them. And God said to them, 'Be fruitful and multiply and fill the earth'* (Gen 1:28). God wants the earth to be filled with creatures made in his image, with human beings. This of course can only achieved by the union of the two sexes, not by same sex unions. Thus in the first command given to the human race, 'Be fruitful and multiply' heterosexual complementarity is implied.

Genesis 2 makes this point even more clearly. The touching story of God seeking for a companion for Adam is so familiar that we may miss its implications. Obviously God creating Eve out of Adam's rib vividly pictures the concept of one-fleshness that exists between man and wife. When people marry, they find the bit that is missing from themselves. But there is more to the story than this.

Genesis 2 pictures God doing everything he can think of for Adam's well being. He puts him in a well-watered garden full of fruit trees. Noting his loneliness God brings the animals to be his companions, but they do not suit. So eventually he creates Eve. But if God was in such a generous mood, why did he not create several Eves? Or even better several extra Adams? According to Genesis this would not have been as good. Monogamy is better than polygamy, and heterosexuality than homosexuality. Man and woman are complementary: they complete each other.

Before leaving Genesis I should make one final point. For Christians, its teaching on sexuality is not obsolete. Jesus explicitly appeals to these passages in establishing his own view of marriage.

Just look at these passages again, and see how he quotes these passages to define God's purpose for the sexes.

Genesis 1:27 (ESV)	Matthew 19:4–5 (ESV)
So God created man in his own image, in the image of God he created him; male and female he created them.	He answered, 'Have you not read that he who *created them* from the beginning made them *male and female*, [5] and said, Therefore a man shall leave his father and his mother and hold fast to his wife, and they shall become one flesh?'
Genesis 2:24 (ESV)	
Therefore a man shall leave his father and his mother and hold fast to his wife, and they shall become one flesh.	

Note too how he takes a comment of the narrator in Genesis as a comment from God himself, *He who created them ... said.* The teaching of Genesis 1 and 2 about sex cannot be dismissed airily by saying, 'That's just the Old Testament'. Jesus himself uses these chapters to define his views, and so should we.

3. The Laws in Leviticus

The Laws in Leviticus 18:22 and 20:13 have already been mentioned. Here I just make two observations about them. First they are very general. Other cultures in the ancient world seem to have tolerated consenting homosexual practice, especially in religion, only condemning it where it involved rape or unequals, such as pederasty. But uniquely the OT condemns both parties, whatever their status, and degree of consent.

Second, the laws against homosexuality are embedded in a catalogue of sexual offences including many types of incest, adultery, bestiality, and also child sacrifice. No one would, I hope, claim that these other sexual offences no longer matter, so why relativise its ban on homosexual acts by saying it is just part of obsolete Leviticus? It is striking that the council of Jerusalem in Acts 15:20–21 seems to be appealing to these very chapters of Leviticus in its ban on sexual immorality.[1] And of course Jesus in summarising the law (Matt 22:39) quotes Leviticus 19:18 *You shall love your neighbour as yourself*, which incidentally comes half-way between the two laws on homosexuality. Is the love-command no longer relevant because it is found in Leviticus? The NT does discard some rules of Leviticus, such as the food laws, but that is because they symbolised and encouraged the separation of Jews as the only people of God. When Gentiles were incorporated in the church, this was misleading; see Acts 10. With all nations eligible to enter the kingdom, all foods could be eaten.[2]

4. The Bible in its Culture

Finally, let me say a word about the cultures the Bible was addressing. It is well known that Greece and Rome tolerated homosexual practices, indeed that many Greeks thought it was part of a young man's education to have sex with an older man. (The ancients discussed how far the practices were the result of upbringing or heredity. In other words the classical world was familiar with the idea of homosexual orientation.[3])

The picture from the ancient orient is not so clear, but again there seems to have been widespread toleration of homosexual acts as long as there was consent. 'In Mesopotamia homosexuality is nowhere condemned as immorality. Anyone could practise it freely, just as anyone could visit a prostitute, provided it was done without violence and without compulsion.'[4]

Thus pre-biblical attitudes to homosexuality were remarkably modern! It is one example among many of how so-called modern attitudes are really ancient paganism raising its head again (other examples are multi-faith worship, abolition of Sunday as universal rest day, abortion, easy divorce). That is why the Bible is still relevant: it spoke to cultures, which in so many respects are similar to our own. We should not be intimidated by the charge of being old-fashioned: it is the so-called liberals who are really taking us back to the dark ages!

5. For Further Reading

Gagnon, Robert A. J., *The Bible and Homosexual Practice* (Nashville: Abingdon Press, 2001). The definitive exegetical treatment by an author with a high view of Scripture's authority, but some unconservative ideas on its composition.

Gagnon, Robert A. J., 'Does the Bible Regard Same-Sex Intercourse as Intrinsically Sinful?' in *Christian Sexuality: Normative and Pastoral Principles* (ed. Russell Saltzman) (Minneapolis: Kirk House, 2003). Unpicks the argument that, while homosexual acts are normally wrong, they are in some cases permissible.

Satinover, Jeffrey, *Homosexuality and the Politics of Truth* (Grand Rapids: Baker Books, 1996). An eye-opener on the health risks of homosexual practice.

Wenham, Gordon J., 'The OT Attitude to Homosexuality', *Expository Times* 102 (1991) pp.359–63.

Wenham, Gordon J., *The Book of Leviticus* (Grand Rapids: Eerdmans, 1979).

Wold, Donald J., *Out of Order: Homosexuality in the Bible and the Ancient Near East* (Grand Rapids: Baker Books, 1998).

Notes

1. H. Conzelmann, *The Acts of the Apostles* (Philadelphia: Fortress Press, 1987) pp.118—19
2. See Gordon J. Wenham, *The Book of Leviticus* (Grand Rapids: Eerdmans, 1979) pp.181—83
3. See Robert Gagnon, *The Bible and Homosexual Practice* (Nashville: Abingdon Press, 2001) pp.380–95
4. Wenham *Expository Times,* 102, 1991, p.360.

Chapter 13

The New Testament Speaks on Same-Sex Eroticism

Edith M. Humphrey

A faithful reading of Scripture is crucial to understanding the issue before us. Scripture is, of course, key to the thinking of the Christian. While we are first of all people of Christ,[1] we are also people of the Book. It is most particularly in the Bible that the supreme glory of our Lord is shown so that the Church can together know the One who is the Truth, and therefore worship together.

The Five-Act Drama

To read Scripture as it is meant to be read, we begin with an understanding of its character.[2] It is not a static deposit of precepts to be mined, but a vibrant collection of books by which the Church is taught, and *by which she is identified.* The story of Scripture can be understood in five great acts[3]: Act 1 tells us about a creator God; Act 2 speaks of his good creation gone askew by death, corruption and sin; Act 3 presents the call of the nation Israel to be a light to the world; Act 4 shows how that calling was fulfilled in a surprising and crucial way in the coming, life, death, resurrection and ascension of Jesus the Christ; Act 5, in which we find ourselves, describes the ongoing life and healing mission of the church through the Holy

Spirit in this world. We await the finale of this drama, but are given, in the Scriptures, wonderful intimations of God's purposes for his people and the entire cosmos.

The Bible came to us in human words, particular to time and place. Some have used this human element to detract from the Bible's authority, and to leash or neutralise its words on difficult subjects. Far be this from us! Rather, we discern in the Bible's many forms – narrative, law, gospel, psalm, epistle, apocalypse – God's coming to be with us, for us and in us. Let us learn this story intimately, so that we can repeat it with human lips to others, and so that we can play our authentic part in it. This 'we' factor is essential! The Scripture implies, and indeed states explicitly, that the Word is heard not privately, but by the whole community, past and present. When we as today's faith community recognise, understand and pass on what has been revealed, we are using the God-given faculty of reason. Our experience and reason are not actual 'authorities' as we understand Scripture or decide about present concerns. Instead, experience (especially the common experience of the church) is our *context*, the place where we receive God's love and wisdom; reason is a 'tool' or means of interpreting what we hear.[4] Under the guidance of the Holy Spirit, and steeped in the written Word of God, we measure the helpfulness of current ideas against a long established understanding of God, the world, and humanity, to see if they stand up to the test.

As members of Christ's body, we are ourselves actors in a divinely conceived drama. While our 'lines' are not wholly prescribed for us, our role is *not* to improvise with abandon, mindless of the story line. In reading the Scriptures together, and by honouring the 'actors' who have gone before us, we keep within our memories and hearts the central, major 'part' in the drama – God's part! As those who have received the Spirit, we will want to share in the mind of Christ, understanding the word personally, but not autonomously or individualistically. The church has, from the beginning, struggled over difficult matters. Her reflection and solemn decisions about ethical and theological matters should be acknowledged as carrying authority for us younger brothers and sisters in the same family.

Together with God's whole church, past and present, we are called to discern God's voice and will, in humility and in confidence that the Holy Spirit was active, is active and will be active in our midst.

The human authors of the Scriptures, moved by the Divine Author, wrote in particular historical contexts. But this fact should not be used as a pretext for bypassing explicit teaching or perspectives which our age finds difficult. Rather, in each case, we are to read all the pertinent texts carefully. Even where we conclude that a passage is particular to a moment in the history of God's people (e.g. prohibition of pork, or head coverings for women), we must respect the underlying theological or ethical truths. Some commands have an enduring claim (e.g. the command not to murder) because they are essentially linked to what has been revealed in the salvation story about the world, our nature, and the nature of God. A faithful reading of Scriptures thus means that we seek to understand how the passages that we are reading, and the questions that we are presently asking, fit into the great forgiving, healing and life-giving drama that has been initiated by God himself.

Jesus, Paul and Human Sexuality

How do the Scriptures speak of human sexuality? We take our cue from the Lord Jesus, who answered questions about human relations by going back to the creation narrative. There we learn that our created sexual differences are key to our identity as human beings. The solemn declaration of Genesis 1:27 stresses both difference and unity: *So God created Adam in his image, in the image of God he created him, male and female he created them.* Sexual distinctions and complementarity are part of God's good (very good! 1:31) creation, though sexuality, along with other facets of human life, has been deeply affected by sin.

So powerful is this communion of male and female that the Bible treats marriage as a mirror of God's love for his people. This understanding of marriage is accentuated in the New Testament, where it is celebrated as an icon of Christ's mysterious love for the Church. Another surprise in the NT is that celibacy comes to be honoured there as a faithful way of celebrating God's goodness. Marriage is a wonderful echo of God's communion with us; celibacy stands as a potent reminder that here not all our needs can be met by another human being, that we are designed for something more than this age. In Matthew 19 and Mark 10 Jesus affirms both celibacy and monogamous marriage – 'What God has joined together let no one put asunder'. Our generation has already seen an assault on God's order by the tragic prevalence of divorce in the Church. It would seem that the tumultuous call for us to 'bless' so-called same-sex 'unions' is a new way of 'putting asunder' what God has joined! Jesus, asked about marriage by his Jewish contemporaries, had no need to speak explicitly about homoeroticism (this had not entered their minds!). The Genesis creation account to which he refers speaks clearly about God's intent for human partnership between male and female.

What Jesus did not need to explicitly address is certainly addressed by his apostle, St Paul, who lived and worked in a Gentile context. Like Jesus, St Paul teaches that there are two Christian lifestyles – marriage is so honourable that a godly partner may hope to influence an unbelieving spouse; singleness is a special gift to the community of the church. In his discussion of marriage in 1 Corinthians, Paul shows how our most intimate inter-relationships may become part of God's medicine. Neither an unlawful heterosexual relationship (such as incest) nor a same-sex union can ultimately fulfil this role, however. To the Corinthians, Paul speaks about 'freedom' in the area of food, but never suggests that incest or other types of sexual immorality could be an authentic expression of freedom in Christ. This is because marriage, by its very character, requires faithful complementarity, not the intimacy of same types, nor casual intimacy. In Christ, our sexuality, expressed in a monogamous physical union, or expressed chastely by single persons in means other than those that are erotic, becomes a powerful factor in helping us to be healed, and to grow up into what we are meant to be. Amidst current assumptions that sexuality is for the purpose of self-gratification, the Church is called to signal to the world an entirely different attitude. Paul was scandalised that the Corinthians were allowing a member of their church to engage in incest (1 Corinthians 5). We

have our own scandal today, and need again to head Paul 's words –
Do not be deceived!

The Silence of Scripture on Homoerotic Expression

Frequently pro-gay lobbies in the Church speak about same-sex erot-icism as if the Bible has little so say regarding it, and as if the biblical writers were naive. They refer to, say, the institution of slavery, and suggest that we have moved beyond the limited understanding of the early Church. These arguments betray an arrogance with regards to the biblical text, and miss the mark.

To begin with, homoerotic behaviour is not analogous to slavery, nor even to the ministry of women in the Church, for that matter. Though some portions of the epistles deal with slavery as a given in the ancient world, 1 Timothy 1:10 lists slave-trading as a vice, and Paul invites slaves to take freedom when they can. What Scriptures have to say about women in ministry is, in my view, complex, but to link this debate with the homosexuality issue is a 'category confu-sion'. As my colleague Robert Gagnon has put it, 'being a woman is not a condition directly linked to sinful behaviour, as is homoerotic desire.'[5] Nor were the biblical writers ignorant of homoeroticism, though they did not express the phenomenon in the psychological language of our day. Indeed, in St Paul's time, there were some who celebrated homoerotic relations as a good thing. Some prominent Gentiles thought and acted this way, but neither the Hebrew people nor the early Christians agreed.

The Bible speaks with one voice about homoerotic activity – from the story of Sodom, to the 'Holiness Code' of Leviticus, to the lists of dark behaviours in the epistles, the word is, 'don't!' The bibli-cal writers adopt a decisive counter-cultural stand against an activity that Greek and Roman poets valorised. It makes little difference whether such sexual behaviour is directed by nature, by nurture, or by a combination of these two. St Paul himself is well aware of the compulsive nature of sin, and puts forth the gospel as God's means of dealing with enslaved expressions of sinfulness as well as sins that are deliberately chosen. Jesus Christ is the centre of healing as well as of acquittal, our Physician as well as our gracious Judge. To say that the apostle would change his mind if he knew the 'findings' of psychological sciences regarding homosexuality is to ignore that the Bible understands well our brokenness and our inclination to destructive behaviour.

Both the Lord Jesus and St Paul, then, describe erotic expression as something blessed by God uniquely within the institution of a faithful marriage. Jesus makes clear that *'from the beginning ...* God made them male and female' and so defines marriage for our confused age as the union of two *differently gendered* human beings. Would that those entrenching law in Canada would listen! In Romans 1:18–32, the Apostle Paul also hearkens back to the creation story (and to the story of the Fall). Read 20–25. Here Paul presents us with a progression: lack of honour and thanksgiving to God has led to ignorance and idolatry, which has led to lustful hearts, which has led to the degradation of the body. The most foundational example of this degradation is homoeroticism (including lesbianism), because this presents a primal breach in the 'male and female' humanity that God declared to be very good. Homoeroticism, then, is pictured as symptomatic of the first rebellion against God. It, along with other symptoms such as covetousness, murder, strife, gossip, deceit, disloyalty and pride, show that human beings have, together, turned away from the God of glory.

Notice that Paul is not talking here about individual persons who have homoerotic desires, but of the phenomenon itself, which is an indicator of our fallen human nature. Together, the human family has turned away from the Creator, refusing to give thanks. We bear, as a race, the wounds of those who will not rejoice in what God has made, and in who we are. Homoerotic activity, because of its character *against nature* does not affirm God's created order as given to us – that is, he has made us 'male and female.' So, in homoerotic action, as in other wrong paths, we show that humanity has forgotten the true God of creation. It seems that the first sin of Adam and Eve was neither pride nor simple disobedience, but lack of gratitude![6] The result is ignorance, idolatry, degradation of body and mind and finally the confusion of evil for good – *they not only do them but even applaud others who practice them* (1 Corinthians 1:32).

In the Corinthian letters, St. Paul singles out sexual immorality as a sin that can affect the whole person, and urges his hearers to flee from it (1 Corinthians 6:18). He also details both active and passive homoerotic activity in a list of vices which the Corinthians *once* practiced before their turn to Christ, and which they must now eschew (1 Corinthians 6:9–11). Some recent commentators, through special pleading, seek to reinterpret or to limit St Paul's use of two terms for homosexual agents those who are *malakoi*, and those who are *arsenokoitai*. The latter term *arsenokoitai* is a word found only in Paul, but clearly a compound derived from the Old Greek Leviticus (Leviticus 20:13) which speaks of 'those who lie with a male as with a female'. The term *malakoi* is less technical, and means literally 'soft ones'; it is found in other Greek documents to refer to those exhibiting various types of sexual indulgence, but often refers explicitly to the passive partner in a homoerotic relationship. Those in doubt should research for themselves the more general cultural use of this term, as documented in, for example, the standard Greek dictionaries.[7] Careful and non-biased studies of these words show that Paul's meaning is all-too-clear. He uses these words to refer to homoerotic behaviour in general, not simply to 'boy prostitution' or 'forced' relations, or 'homosexual activity between naturally heterosexual partners', as some[8] want to argue.

The Church's Understanding

In line with the New Testament, early Christian communities retained this same view regarding sexual immorality, including same-sex erotic activity. Right up through to the mid-twentieth century, Christian theologians including Chrysostom, Augustine, Aquinas, Calvin and Karl Barth[9] have understood homoerotic behaviour as a sign of the disruption of the good created order[10] and as a sin that calls for repentance, restoration and healing.

Sometimes, of course, leaders in the Church have fallen prey to self-justification, and have vilified those engaging in same-sex sin as worse than those indulging in other sins. The New Testament is quick to correct us if we are self-righteous, without softening its words against homoerotic behaviour itself. *And such* said St Paul, *were some of you. But you have been washed.*

(Please let me add a quick word on what 'healing' might entail – for some, it may well mean reorientation, and we have friends who have testified to this; for others, celibacy will be the path of healing, offering a path of witness to many who think that sexual expression is a necessity for a fulfilled life. I am profoundly grateful to my brothers and sisters in Christ who struggle with same-sex desire but witness in their lives to the sufficiency of Christ; they remind me that we cannot yet imagine all that God has in store for us, and that his grace is sufficient to meet us in our brokenness. Nor will he leave us there – we await 'temples' that will take up into glory these 'tents' in which we now dwell, as Paul anticipates in 2 Corinthians 5.)

Thus we can summarize the Church's faithful reading of the Scripture in this way: those struggling with homoeroticism are to be included in the community of faith, along with the rest of us sinners. God's grace is extended to all. However, anyone who joins such the household of God should know that it is a place of transformation, discipline, and learning – *not a place to be falsely comforted or indulged.*[11] Christ's body is to be truly inclusive, extending to all her members the benefits of membership, including confession, repentance, forgiveness and healing. Jesus' gospel remains: Repent, for the rule of God is at hand!

A House Divided

Dietrich Bonhoeffer, who learned the depth of God's grace in a dark time, speaks powerfully to us about ethics, reality and truth: 'If one is to say how a thing really is, *i.e.* if one is to speak truthfully, one's gaze and one's thought must be directed towards the way in which the real exists in God and through God and for God.'[12] Bonhoeffer thus sends us back to Romans 1 and further back to Genesis 1 through 3, that we might see God's world, the creation, and human sexuality as they really are. God's creation is good, though flawed: his purpose is to redeem, heal and glorify it.

But there are some who will not see it this way. Instead they want us to put skewed human experience in place of Jesus, Paul and the historic Church, and to declare that we have transcended the clear voice of Scripture on this issue. In place of the communion of saints and the teaching of the apostles they put a new gospel of so-called inclusivity, and tell us to bless what needs to be healed. What would it mean for the Anglican communion to acknowledge a person involved in same-sex eroticism as a godly example? What would it mean to bless same-sex erotic arrangements? It would be to declare that these so-called 'unions' are in themselves pictures or icons of God's love, to say that they display the salvation story, to rejoice that that they are glorified or taken up into God's own actions and being.[13] It would be to declare that they have a significant and fruitful part in creation, and that they are symbols of the in-breaking and coming rule of God, in which the Church now shares and in which we will eventually participate fully. It would be to 'speak a good word' about this sort of relationship, explicitly declaring it to be a condition in which the way of the cross and the way of new life come together. Precisely here, the Church would be saying, you can see the love of God in human form, and the glory of humanity. It would be to name God as the one who blesses an act for which in fact *repentance* is required. So we would replace God with an idol and so we would rend the Church. What will the Church do when it prays against itself? A house divided cannot stand.

The prophet Jeremiah knew a day like ours.

> They have treated the wound of my people carelessly, saying, 'Peace, peace,' when there is no peace.
>
> Thus says the LORD: Stand at the crossroads, and look and ask for the ancient paths, where the good way lies, and walk in it, and find rest for your souls. But they said, 'We will not walk in it.' (Jeremiah 6:14, 16)
>
> How can you say, 'We are wise, and the law of the LORD is with us,' when, in fact, the false pen of the scribes has made it into a lie? The wise shall be put to shame, and taken, since they have rejected the word of the Lord, what wisdom is there in them?

*They have treated the wound of my people carelessly, saying,
'Peace, peace,' when there is no peace. For the hurt of my poor
people I am hurt, I mourn, and dismay has taken hold of me.
Is there no balm in Gilead? Is there no physician there? (Jeremiah
8:8, 11, 22)*

*You therefore, beloved, beware that you are not carried away
with the error of the lawless and lose your own stability ... [Rather]
be attentive to the [word] as to a lamp shining in a dark place*
(2 Peter 3:17; 2 Peter 2:19b).

Cited texts and Further Reading Pertaining to Same-Sex Eroticism

Barth, Karl, *Church Dogmatics* 111.4 (Edinburgh: T & T Clark, 1957).

Barth, Karl, *Romans*, tr. E. C. Hoskyns (Oxford: Oxford University Press, 1933).

Bonhoeffer, Dietrich, *Ethics*, tr. Nevil Horton Smith, ed. E. Rethge (London: SCM Press, 1955).

Boswell, John, *Christianity, Social Tolerance and Homosexuality* (Chicago: Chicago University Press, 1981).

Countryman, L. William, *Dirt, Greed and Sex: Sexual Ethics in the New Testament and Their Implications for Today* (London: SCM Press, 1989, new ed. 2001).

Evdokimov, Paul, *The Sacrament of Love*: *The Nuptial Mystery in the Light of the Orthodox Tradition*, French original 1952, tr. A. P. Gythiel and F. Steadman (Crestwood, N.Y.: St. Vladimir's Press, 1985).

Evdokimov, Paul, *Woman and the Salvation of the World: A Christian Anthropology on the Charisms of Woman*, tr. A. P. Gythiel (Crestwood, NY: St. Vladimir's Press, tr. 1994).

Gagnon, Robert A. J., *The Bible and Homosexual Practice: Texts and Hermeneutics* (Nashville: Abingdon, 2001).

Gagnon, Robert A. J and Dan O. Via, *Homosexuality and the Bible: Two Views* (Minneapolis: Fortress Press, 2003).

Harakas, S., *Contemporary Moral Issues Facing the Orthodox Christian* (Minneapolis: Light and Life, 1982).

Hays, Richard, 'Relations Natural and Unnatural: A Response to John Boswell's Exegesis of Romans 1,' *Journal of Religious Ethics* 14 (1986), pp.184–215.

Hays, Richard, 'Awaiting the Redemption of Our Bodies,' in ed. J. S. Siker, *Homosexuality in the Church*: *Both Sides of the Debate* (Louisville, KY: Westminster/John Knox, 1994) pp.3–17.

Hays, Richard, *The Moral Vision of the New Testament: A Contemporary Introduction to NT Ethics* (San Francisco: HarperSanFranciso 1996).

Humphrey, Edith M., 'Four Papers in the Service of New Westminster Diocese,' www.augustinecollege.org/papers.htm.

Humphrey, Edith M., 'Same-Sex Eroticism and the Church: Classical Approaches and Responses', in *The Homosexual Debate*: *Faith Seeking Understanding*, ed. Catherine Sider Hamilton (Toronto: ABC, 2003, 37–96).

Humphrey, Edith M., 'Why this Issue?' www.praverbook.ca/articles/c3w.htm

Hurtado, Larry, 'The Bible and Same-Sex Erotic Relations,' *Crux* 32 (1996).

Melton, J. G., *The Churches Speak on Homosexuality* (Detroit: Gale, 1991).

Moberley, Elizabeth, *Homosexuality*: *A New Christian Ethic* (Cambridge: James Clarke and Co., 1983).

Nicolosi, J., *Reparative Therapy of Male Homosexuality* (Northvale, NJ: Jason Aronson, Inc., 1991).

Reisman J. A. et at, *Kinsey, Sex and Fraud* (Layfayette, LA: Lochinvar-Huntingdon House, 1990).

Satinover, Jeffrey, *Homosexuality and the Politics of Troth* (Grand Rapids: Baker, 1996).

Schmernann, Alexander, *For the Life of the World; Sacraments and Orthodoxy* (Crestwood, NY: St Vladimir's Press, 1995).

Scroggs, Robin, *The New Testament and Homosexuality: Contextual Background for Contemporary Debate* (Philadelphia: Fortress, 1983).

Siker, J. S., ed., *Homosexuality in the Church: Both Sides of the Debate* (Louisville, KY: Westminster/John Knox, 1994).

Sider Hamilton, Catherine, *The Homosexuality Debate: Faith Seeking Understanding* (Toronto: ABC Press, 1993).

Soards, Marion, *Scripture and Homosexuality; Biblical Authority and the Church Today* (Louisville, KY: Westminster/John Knox, 1995).

Ware, Kallistos, *The Orthodox Church*, revised edition (Baltimore: Penguin, 1996).

Wright, D. F.,'Homosexuality,' in Ferguson, E. ed., *Encyclopedia of Early Christianity*, 2nd ed., Vol.1 (New York: Garland Publishing, 1997) p.542.

Wright, D. F.,'Homosexuality' in *Dictionary of Paul and his Letters*, eds. G. F . Hawthorne and R. P. Martin (Downer's Grove, IL: InterVarsity Press, 1993).

Wright, N. T., *The New Testament and the People of God* (Minneapolis: Fortress Press, 1992).

Notes

1. The twentieth century stand-off between liberalism and fundamentalism (taken in its strict sense) has tended to skew the perspective of confessing Christians regarding the centre of the Christian community. John Barton *(People of the Book* [Louisville, KY: Westminster/John Knox Press, 1988]) points out that, although the Qu'ran honours Christians and Jews, as well as Muslims, with the designation 'People of the Book,' this is more precise of Judaism and Islam than it is of Christianity. Though we may not follow Barton in all of his deliberations, it is clear that he is right in one respect: 'the Word' is first of all the second Person of the Trinity, incarnate in Jesus Christ; secondarily, it is the holy collection known to us as the Bible. To put the personal Word rather than the written Word in the central place, as

the 'holy of holies' is not to denigrate the Scriptures, but to understand their essential, authoritative, and God-given place. The One who is himself the Word, the Way, Truth and Life, is both illumined by the Scriptures, and shows us how to approach them.

2. For a deeper discussion of these issues, see Edith Humphrey, '*Kairos* and *Chronos*: Meditations on Revelation, God's Word and God's World,' in *Fanning the Flame*: *Bible, Cross and Mission*, ed. Gardner, Wright and Green (Grand Rapids: Zondervan, 2003, pp.99–116).

3. The Bible as presenting an underlying Divine-human drama in Five Acts is suggested to us by the work of N. T. Wright, first in 'How Can the Bible Be Authoritative?' *Vox Evangelica* 21:7–32, and more recently in *The New Testament and the People of God* (Minneapolis: Fortress, 1992, pp.141–43).

4. The so-called 'Wesleyan quadrilateral' seems to have replaced the so-called Anglican 'three-legged stool' by many theologians, across denominational lines. From the time of the Enlightenment on, 'reason' was frequently (mis)used *over against* the Scriptures, as rationalists debated what could be reasonably believed (say, in terms of the mighty acts of God). Today there is a new challenge in the much-celebrated 'quadrilateral' of 'authorities': Wesley, though utterly concerned about experience in a time of arid dogmatism, would not have recognised the way that it is being appealed to as a trump-card in revisionist theology today. Evangelicals and charismatics in the Anglican communion may be particularly susceptible to the Trojan horse of 'experience' being introduced as a fourth and frequently final 'authority' in significant current debates, because of their insistence upon personal knowledge of the Lord. We do well to keep things in their proper place: let us cherish our personal and corporate experience of the Way and the Christian life, while remembering that the Lord himself, as illuminated by the Scriptures, and proclaimed in the

traditional creeds, is our authority and the One whom we adore.

5. Robert Gagnon and Dan O. Via, *Homosexuality and the Bible*: *Two Views* (Minneapolis: Augsburg Fortress, 2003) p.46.

6. Alexander Schmemann, *For the Life of the World*: *Sacraments and Orthodoxy* (first edition 1963, second expanded edition originally 1973; Crestwood, N.Y.: St. Vladimir's Press, 2000) p.16 ff.

7. e.g. Liddell & Scott or Bauer-Amdt-Gingrich-Danker.

8. See, among others, the tendentious arguments of John Eoswell, *Christianity, Social Tolerance and Homosexuality*, 1981; Robin Scroggs, *The New Testament and Homosexuality: Contextual Background for Contemporary Debate*, Philadelphia: Fortress, 1983; and L. William Countryman, *Dirt, Greed and Sex: Sexual Ethics in the New Testament and Their Implications for Today*, 1989, new ed. 2001. They are briefly and well refuted by Richard Hays in his 'Relations Natural and Unnatural: A Response to John Eoswell's *Exegesis of Romans 1*,' *Journal of Religious Ethics* 14, 1986, pp. 184–215.

9. Recently, George Hunsinger, *Presbyterian Outlook*, March 13 and May 17, 2002, has speculated that the late Barth may have changed his views. A careful analysis of the documents that he cites does not in fact indicate that Barth *reversed* his opinion, but that he was not satisfied with the form of his arguments as expressed in the Dogmatics. For more detail, see Edith M. Humphrey, 'Same-Sex Eroticism and the Church: Classical Approaches and Responses, in *The Homosexual Debate*: *Faith Seeking Understanding*, ed. Catherine Sider Hamilton (Toronto: ABC, 2003) p.88, footnote 37.

10. For a more detailed description and analysis of these classical writers, see Edith M. Humphrey, 'Same-Sex Eroticism and the Church: Classical Approaches and Responses, in

The Homosexual Debate: *Faith Seeking Understanding*, pp. 37–90.

11. These are the words of 'Gary', a pseudonym for the friend of NT scholar Richard Hays. Gary came to a classical understanding of biblical sexuality while afflicted with AIDS, and in study with Hays. Read the entire story, as written after Gary's death, by Hays in 'Awaiting the Redemption of Our Bodies,' in ed. J. S. Siker, *Homosexuality in the Church*: *Both Sides of the Debate* (Louisville, KY: Westminster/John Knox, 1994) pp. 3–17 and The *Moral Vision of the New Testament*: *A Contemporary Introduction to NT Ethics* (San Francisco: HarperSanFrancisco, 1996) p.380 ff.

12. Dietrich Bonhoeffer, *Ethics*, tr. Nevil Horton Smith, ed. E. Rethge (London: SCM Press, 1955) p. 365.

13. For a more precise critique of a suggested ceremony, see the final paper in Edith M. Humphrey, 'Four Papers in the Service of New Westminster Diocese,' *www.augustinecollege. org/papers.htm*. These four papers also afford the reader a more detailed discussion of all the issues sketched in this NEAC address.

Conference Addresses

Conference Addresses

Most Revd and Rt Hon Dr Rowan Williams is the Archbishop of Canterbury

Rt Revd James Jones is the Bishop of Liverpool

Most Revd and Rt Hon Dr David Hope is the Archbishop of York

Revd Professor Alister McGrath is Principal of Wycliffe Hall, Oxford

Rt Revd Wallace Benn is the Bishop of Lewes and President of the Church of England Evangelical Council

Letter from the NEAC4 Steering Committee to Anglicans in North America

Chapter 14

Opening Greeting

The Most Revd and Rt Hon Dr Rowan Williams, Archbishop of Canterbury

Thank you all for such a generous welcome. It's a great pleasure to be here not simply because it's a great pleasure to be off the motorway. I'm only sorry that this is such a short visit; I hope to be able to sit and listen a bit while I'm here as well, but I have unfortunately to go back to London later tonight.

As you can imagine I have thought quite a bit about what I might say by way of greeting today and I heroically resisted the temptation to give you a Bible study based on the verse from the prayer book translation of Psalm 71, 'I am become as it were a monster unto many.' And I thought instead that what I would do is simply to talk to you about three words which are the focus of why you are here, why we are here – Bible, Cross, Mission. Trying to put those words in a context, trying to make some connections between them, trying to bring to mind what it is that holds us here together and drives us forward.

I take it to be an evangelical is among many other things to take the Reformation seriously and the first principle of the Reformation was that the believer must listen to God. And the trouble is because of our fallen state, our minds shy away from listening; and sin infects our institutions as well as our minds, so that even the Church can become a huge conspiracy to avoid listening to God.

But God has not left himself without living witness; and this conference is surely an exercise in attending to and celebrating God's witness to himself as we receive it in the Church. So I'm going to spend a few minutes reflecting with you specifically on how the three focal topics of this conference concentrate our minds and hearts on listening to God, to God bearing witness to himself.

But there is one point to note first though. When God speaks, when God witnesses to himself, he doesn't first tell us things in our world: he first tells us who he is. The eternal Word of God is the Son, 'the exact likeness of God's own being' as Hebrews 1:3 says. God eternally says who he is in the divine person who became flesh in Jesus of Nazareth, and this is the foundation of all God's speaking in history and revelation. In other words, as we listen to hear God in Bible, Cross and Mission, we listen first so as to hear God telling us who he is.

He tells us who he is in Scripture – in the whole history of his interaction with the world and especially the human world and especially the people he chooses. He tells us that he is a God who creates the world out of sheer loving abundance, not out of necessity, to see his own beauty and goodness reflected in it. He tells us that he is a God who makes and keeps promises, who founds a whole nation on the bare fact of his choice and promise and commitment. He tells us that he is a God with whom we cannot live if we break that chosen community by injustice, greed and self-regard. And he tells us that the promise first made to the ancestors was greater than they ever knew, because it was a promise to be with them in an unimaginable way, as a human being among human beings, as Emmanuel, God with us; and that once the covenant is revolutionised by the coming of Emmanuel, God with us, his promise is to be with all his children, from every tribe and tongue, to the end of the age.

But the way the Bible tells us who God is is sharply concentrated on the one event in which God's witness to himself is most drastic, most astonishing and shocking, most mysterious. Emmanuel, God with us, not only shares our humanity in general. He shares our death and carries the condemnation we have earned by our sin; he endures the depth of forsakenness by God so that the way may be opened to life for us. In the cross, God tells us who he is, tells us that he is a God who will shrink from no cost for our sake, a God who is free not only to be God in heaven, in glory and bliss, but to be God in human pain and dread so as to lead us out of those prisons. A God who, in the great words of the eucharistic prayer of St Basil, 'has left nothing undone', before whom no door of guilt or sorrow is locked, who has descended and ascended so that he might fill all things (Ephesians 4:10).

God tells us who he is in Scripture. God tells us who he is in the cross. And while we might find it odd at first hearing to think of God as telling us who he is in mission, the truth is that, because God in Christ has 'filled all things' in this way, when we proclaim and share the news of our promise-keeping God who has vowed to be with us always, we say that God is witnessing to his own action, through the words and actions we perform. God's breath, God's Spirit, breathed into us gives us the freedom to act in and for the Risen Jesus. Mission assumes that there is nowhere where God, the God of Jesus Christ, is irrelevant, that there is no person or society he cannot transform. And so mission tells us who God is by telling us that, wherever we are, he has gone before us to prepare the way.

We're here, then, I hope, to listen to God telling us who he is, thinking about Bible, Cross and Mission so that we can hear again what is his nature and his name. Only so, as every generation of Christians has recognised, will we discover who we are – created by love, ruined by sin, forgiven and transfigured by suffering and sacrifice and the gift of the Spirit, so that it is given to us to be with Jesus where he is.

That's all I'm here to say. I pray this gathering will renew everyone's eagerness to listen to God speaking his nature and his name, in such a way that others will be able to hear and believe and give thanks. So we pray for that to be God's gift to us in the days ahead.

© Rowan Williams 2003

Chapter 15

Opening Address

James Jones, the Bishop of Liverpool

Bishop James spoke immediately after the opening greeting from the Archbishop of Canterbury. He welcomed him warmly to the Congress, and then turned to the principal theme of his address.

In this conference we renew our obedience to the Great Commission to go into all the world in the power of the Spirit to enable others to become learners of Christ with us and to teach all that he commanded. This is no easy task. The complexities of today's world could never have been imagined by the biblical authors of yesterday. Learning the mind of Christ and discerning God's will for our modern moral dilemmas calls for patient study and humility and a global perspective.

We do this with reference to the authority of Scripture, to the lessons of tradition and to the voice of reason which is informed by the experience of contemporary culture. As evangelicals we hold that in this three-fold reference there is a primacy to the Authority of Scripture.

I hesitate to use the world 'evangelical'. This is not because I do not associate myself with the tradition unashamedly but because I am so aware of the negative way in which the word is used today.

Recently a woman of evangelical faith was being interviewed for a teaching post in one of our church primary schools. She was, as it happened, the best candidate. However, the LEA representative in approving the appointment reported 'she was not an evangelical, her faith just flowed from her so naturally and joyfully.'

I remember in the previous Archbishop of York's staff meeting listening to another bishop describe the merits of an able vicar then adding, 'He's an evangelical *but* he's very nice!'

There are all sorts of reasons for this negative public perception. Some of it may be deserved but some of it we have no control over. Yet conscious of our critics we do well to hold fast to the Scriptures and the Lord's timeless message:

> *What does the Lord require of you*
> *but to do justice, and to love mercy*
> *and to walk humbly with your God?*

Humility is not an optional virtue. It is a divine imperative that must mark our gathering. It must shape our relationship with God, our relationships with each other including other Christian traditions and our relationship with the world at large.

Ever since I was a student William Wilberforce has been my hero. He was an evangelical Christian whose radical political action was inspired by the Scriptures. One of the joys of becoming Bishop of Hull was discovering that Wilberforce had been its Member of Parliament.

Wilberforce was able to read the Bible, uncluttered by the cultural baggage that blinded others to God's mind, and to see the biblical principles that led to the abolition of the slave trade and slavery itself. He swam strenuously against the tide, culturally and economically. He was told he 'would ruin the empire', but he persisted with principles inspired by evangelical faith and prevailed. Not because public opinion changed or because fellow members were persuaded. But because in God's providence MPs from Ireland were added to Parliament and gave the abolitionists the majority necessary to change the world.

The historian Kathleen Heasman has estimated that three-quarters of the social reform of the nineteenth century was directly attributable to evangelical Christianity. That is our heritage.

The world has, of course, changed. Yet that determination to connect the Word and the World in both the private and public domain remains, or ought to remain, a hallmark of evangelical faith. When critics belittle the evangelical tradition I want to remind them that we stand not in the same frame as transatlantic televangelists but in the noble tradition of Wilberforce and Shaftsbury and Cranmer.

There are some who would argue that evangelicalism is an aberration on the canvass of English Christianity. Yet the protestant and puritan emphases on the Word had a dramatic effect not just on the church but upon the politics of England and consequently the English-speaking world. Jeremy Paxman in his book *The English* writes, 'the power of the Word extended much further. By offering a direct relationship with God, unmediated by popes or bishops, the common language of devotion gave the individual all sorts of rights he might never have otherwise thought he had.' Paxman adds that the Reformation with its iconoclasm also changed the culture of England. 'Here was the replacement of the visual with the verbal ... The English not only came to a new way of appreciating the Word, they came to an appreciation of Words.'

The English are a people of the Word which is why even in the face of an audio-visual culture evangelicalism defies the media obituaries of Christianity and continues to grow.

Yet as we grow, we acknowledge the diversity of Anglicanism and value the biblical insights of other traditions.

For a large part of the twentieth century, while evangelicalism had forgotten the nineteenth century heritage of Wilberforce and Shaftsbury, it was the liberal tradition that upheld the biblical principles of social justice in the Kingdom of God. And in the same period it was the Catholic tradition that saw more clearly than most of us (with the exception of Colin Buchanan!) that liturgy is the defining expression of theology and doctrine.

With humility we need, notwithstanding our present differences, to recognise when other traditions have read and acted upon the Scriptures more faithfully than we have. My hope for this conference is that we will engage in three conversations. With each other – we are a much more diverse company than people outside our tradition imagine. And rightly so, for throughout the worldwide Anglican communion we are engaging with different cultures and this will be reflected necessarily in our different emphases. With other traditions – listening and learning, testifying and teaching with humility what God has revealed. With the world at large – engaging privately and publicly in debates about values and vision, structures and strategies on the future of the earth. NEAC4 is not about defining a sect; it is about engaging with a continually reforming church as we respond to the Mission of God in the World. In all of this our primary text and authoritative script is the Bible, however incomprehensible that may be to the outside world.

One of our confidences in the Scriptures is this – and it is a Reformation principle – that you do not need a special caste of people to interpret it. Put it into the vernacular and let the Bible speak. It is my testimony and that of many that reading the Scriptures has brought us heart to heart, mind to mind with God. Sometimes in a dramatic way, touching our deepest emotions. Through the Spirit we have been changed by the encounter. Not all the time, not often so dramatically but sufficiently to know, with the apostle, here are 'the words of eternal life'.

As we study the Bible we must be open to what further truth may break upon us from the Scriptures. Speaking personally, during my study leave last year I took the theme 'Jesus and the Earth – a rereading of the Gospels with an environmental awareness.' I approached it with the question: if the environment is so important why do Christians go mainly to the Old Testament? Is there nothing in the Gospels about the earth? Well, I now believe there is! Except that we seldom see it because of the baggage that we bring to the text. For example, like many evangelicals I preach often on the cross and as often on the Temple Curtain, torn from top to bottom. But I hardly mention the earth and its quaking. Nor the earth quaking again at the Resurrection. Yet the earth is more eloquent than the curtain.

It gladdened my heart when I went to see John Stott about what I might say today. He urged us as evangelicals, 'to be open to what further truth may break upon us from Scripture'. I love the scent of creativity and the sense of adventure in such a humble attitude to the authority of Scripture. Hopefully, our gathering here in Blackpool will be marked by such creativity and adventure as we engage seriously with the Bible.

The second great theme of the Congress is the Cross. Michael Ramsey, at the Keele Conference in 1967, spoke of the Lordship of Jesus like this: 'So the crux of the ministry of Jesus ... is that Jesus must in obedience to the Father's purposes concentrate not upon those beneficent works, which are of course near to his heart of compassion, but upon the paramount theme of sin and the forgiveness and conquest of sin. It is here that the supreme battle of the Kingdom of God must be fought.'[1]

Now this doctrine of an objective atonement is not the preserve of evangelicalism but it is one of the essentials of evangelicalism. Archbishop Ramsey touched on something else of importance, 'Our power so to serve God is always rooted in our status as men and women who receive the miracle of divine forgiveness. Without the centrality of the Cross the Church may misunderstand its doctrine, its own life, and the secret of its power.'

The secret of its power! As we engage with the Bible and the Cross in this conference this is not to be some stagnant pool or some sterile clinic – this is to be a place of God's presence and power, where we ourselves are changed by the Spirit through our own encounter with the Word – the Word written and the Word crucified, risen and ascended.

Within the evangelical tradition this transformation has been most eloquently expressed in the call to Holiness. My predecessor J. C. Ryle wrote the classic evangelical treatise on 'Holiness'. I read it on my ordination retreat alongside Graham Greene's *The Power and the Glory*. In Greene's novel there's a haunting comment that, 'There is always one moment in childhood when the door opens and lets the future in'. Our tradition's noted work with children and young people echoes that Jesuit saying, 'Give me a child until he is seven and I will give you the man.'

The encounter with Christ, the Word incarnate, is the opening of a door onto a path that leads steadfastly to personal holiness. I love J. C. Ryle's images of sanctification

> When an eagle is happy in an iron cage, when a sheep is happy
> in the water, when an owl is happy in the blaze of noonday sun,
> when a fish is happy on the dry land – then, and not till then, will
> I admit that the unsanctified man could be happy in heaven.

Ryle's sights were clearly on heaven but his focus was very much
on the earth as he engaged in the contemporary political and social
justice issues of Liverpool such as child poverty and unemployment.
This part of his heritage is not as well remembered.

My own experiences in Hull and Liverpool, immersed in the realities of urban mission, have informed and transformed my reading of
the Scriptures. I believe there is an inextricable link between the doctrine of *just*ification by faith and acting *just*ly in God's world. How
can a person be reconciled through the Cross to the God of justice
and mercy without at the same time being caught up in the dynamic
of God's action in the world to do justice and act mercifully.

How does God act in the world? What do the Scriptures say?
With justice and mercy. What is required of God's people? What
do the Scriptures say? 'To *do* justice and to *love* mercy'. Whenever
the evangelical tradition has allowed a wedge to be driven between
justification by faith and acting justly, between personal salvation
and social justice, it has become sub-biblical.

Never has this biblical connection between the personal and the
social, the private and public been so timely to affirm.

The earth faces challenges the magnitude of which are unique
in its history. Previously human actions were but the trifles of flies
ranged against the forces of nature. That is all now reversed. Human
actions are literally changing the balances within creation. An Indian
theologian, R. L. Sarkar, has written

> In the remote past, human actions were trivial when set against
> the dominant processes of nature. No longer is this so. The
> human species now influences the fundamental processes of
> the planet. Ozone depletion, worldwide pollution, and climate
> change are testimonies to our power.

The Scriptures tell us that the earth is the Lord's and everything
in it. The Scriptures tell us that all has come into being *through* and

for Christ. Never has so much theology hung upon two such small prepositions!

The environment, biotechnology, global poverty, international governance, human sexuality, the nurture of children are all raising fundamental questions about how we should then live. Into these debates the Bible speaks. As evangelicals we must read the Scriptures and distil from its pages moral principles.

The Bible, inspired and with authority, urges us to walk humbly and to approach the world with a sense of moral awe. It is this which seems so lacking in our contemporary world where irreversible decisions are taken without due care and attention to their ethical quality and long-term consequences. We urgently need to recover to our public debates the sense of moral awe which is characterised by four hallmarks. First, all our actions spring from and shape our characters. Secondly, all our actions have consequences, individually and socially. Thirdly, all our actions will be judged by future generations. Fourthly, we are all responsible for our actions to the source of our moral intuition.

I believe that this sense of moral awe can be a bridge, rather like Paul's Areopagan altar, with our culture, enabling us to enter into dialogue and public debate with those beyond the boundary of the Christian faith.

As we engage in this debate, the Bible is foundational, for here God has spoken. From what reason does God speak? From love. For what purpose does he speak? For salvation. You see, 'The Bible, Cross and Mission' are not just three conference themes dreamed up – albeit after much discussion! – by a planning committee. Bible, Cross and Mission are the *signs* of God's love in and for the world. They form a unique trinity:

The Bible	he communicates because he longs to draw us into communion with himself
The Cross	he himself makes the atonement, the communion which we are incapable of making
Mission	his own self-sending, the model of our being sent, is compelled by his love for the world.

'Bible, Cross and Mission' – Trinitarian tokens of the love of the Triune God, Father, Son and Holy Spirit. These are themes to capture our imagination, to stir our heart and to engage with the world globally.

In conclusion, I quote from Matthew Parris's autobiography. He grew up in Africa and witnessed the work of Christian missionaries. Although an atheist he writes:

> I began to understand why eyes looked brighter and steps lighter in those areas where a missionary was at work. Because Christianity teaches a direct personal relationship, bypassing hierarchy and tribe, with God it can represent a release to those oppressed by their tribe and its panoply of brooding and often vengeful spirits. I do not myself believe in God but can still see how Christian monotheism can act to liberate.

One of the greatest challenges that Christians face from our contemporary culture is to demonstrate by the quality of our being and doing that this spiritual and liberating transformation is not simply a subjective and psychological event, but is real, objective and rooted in the God of love who has spoken to us through his Son and reveals himself to his beloved world through the Bible, by the Cross and in Mission.

Notes

1. Published in *The Churchman*, vol. 81 no. 2, Summer 1967, pp. 89–94.

Chapter 16

Stop, Look and Listen

Dr David Hope, Archbishop of York

One hundred and twenty four years ago in 1879 in his own introduction to his book *Holiness* John Charles Ryle wrote this – 'I have had a deep conviction for many years that practical holiness and entire self-consecration to God are not sufficiently attended to by modern Christians in this country. Politics or controversy, or party spirit, or worldliness, have eaten out the heart of lively piety in too many of us'. Those words could easily have been written today – for they are just as relevant and pertinent not simply for those who describe themselves as evangelical Christians but for each and every Christian person quite regardless of church or denomination.

So it was in order to address this situation that Ryle began what he described as his God-given duty – and pulling no punches – to set before his readers the uncompromising demands of what an Anglican divine in an earlier age had described as 'a serious call to a devout and holy life'. And there is very clear evidence that the evangelical forebears took this call very seriously indeed. Charles Simeon – you will remember as the one who placed the quotation 'Sir, we would see Jesus' on his pulpit in Cambridge to remind preachers of their primary task in their preaching – rose at 4 a.m. to give four hours to prayer and Bible study. William Grimshaw – an evangelical clergyman of the eighteenth century and one-time Vicar of Haworth in Yorkshire whose parishioners he describes as 'stubborn, independent and inured to hardship' – again rising early to attend to his prayers and Bible study wrote as follows, 'As soon as you awake in the morning employ an hour in five things: bless God for the mercies of the past night; praise Him for a new day, and pray for the blessing of it; examine well your own hearts; meditate upon some serious spiritual subject; and lastly plan out the business of the day'. We are told that he always dressed singing a hymn, spent a further half hour in reading his Bible in his study and then went on to lead family worship. Prayer punctuated the rest of the day '... undress and lie down with prayer,' he continued, 'and never fall asleep with an unforgiven sin upon your conscience'.

He describes meditation – I believe very helpfully – as 'the soul's chewing', a resonance surely of the Cranmerian Collect that we may 'read, mark, learn and inwardly digest God's holy Word'. And I just wonder how much soul's chewing is done by each one of us present this evening? Quite frankly when I read such accounts and I stop and think about myself, I am put to shame at the paucity of my own commitment to such 'soul's chewing' and even then often the begrudging nature of it. The truth is that we have become altogether too busy and too noisy, too wordy and too chatty. Does our worship really have to be wall to wall words, music and action? Do our prayer meetings and Bible study groups have to be a series of monologues that the Lord will just do this, that or the other thing? Simply looking through the programme at the Winter Gardens for this conference left me feeling quite exhausted – go straight to your next forum location ... visit the bookstall, exhibition and ICC recording stand ... don't forget to pick up your tapes and your videos ... and so on. Where is the stillness, the silence, the listening – what used to be termed among evangelicals the quiet time? Are we still capable of being still and quiet or have we become so conformed to the ways of this world that we are no longer able to hear that Word of God – that Word which in the Epistle to the Hebrews 'is living and active, sharper than any two-edged sword, piercing until it divides soul from spirit, joints from marrow; able to judge the thoughts and intentions of the heart before Him no creature is hidden all are naked and laid bare to the eyes of the One to whom we must render an account'.

And it's not just evangelicals, it is all of us who increasingly seem to be unable to carve out this quiet time so essential to our soul's health. We rightly boast of our biblical inheritance, of our biblical foundation roots and basis. Yet how seriously do we take not simply the reading of the Bible day by day – even if we take that seriously – but what the monastic tradition describes as 'lectio divina' – the spiritual reading of the Bible.

It is a Roman Catholic author, Henri Nouwen in his powerful little book *The Way of the Heart*, who writes, 'I would like to stress the importance of silence in the ways ministers and churches organise their lives and those of others. In a society in which entertainment and distraction are such important preoccupations ministers and churches are also tempted to join the ranks of those who consider it their primary task to keep other people busy. It's easy to perceive the young and the elderly as people who need to be kept off the streets or on the streets and ministers frequently find themselves in fierce competition with people and institutions who offer something more exciting to do than they do. But our task is the opposite of distraction. Our task is to help people concentrate on the real but often hidden event of God's active presence in their lives. Hence the question that must guide all our organising activity in a parish is not how to keep people busy but how to keep them from being so busy that they can no longer hear the voice and Word of God who speaks in silence'.

One of the very remarkable events which has taken place now for two years at Ampleforth Abbey has been a gathering of some four or five hundred Christian people of widely differing churches and denominations and groups on a Saturday in July simply to read and reflect on the Bible together. One passage of Scripture only has been our food and our nourishment for the day – a day of silence and sharing – a day of openness to God's word and each other – a day when difference and diversity is transformed by God's Word and God's grace as together we are held in the transforming power of the Holy Spirit – a day which has enabled us to go out each with a deeper and more profound respect for each other and our differing views and opinions precisely because we have together been prepared to stop and look and listen. But then small wonder if you actually take the trouble to ponder more deeply those mighty acts of God set out for us in the Scriptures themselves.

You will recall that when Moses is fleeing from Pharaoh and the Israelites are being pursued by the overwhelming force of the Egyptian armies – and with the prospect of the Red Sea before them and with the people complaining, *what have you done to us bringing us out of Egypt?* Moses didn't call a conference or a meeting – a synod or a standing committee – what does he do? He says to the people, *Do not be afraid, stand still, stand firm and see the deliverance that the Lord will accomplish for you today ... the Lord will fight for you, you have only to be still.*

Again in the mighty act of God in the birth of Jesus Christ, it was when all things were in quiet silence that the almighty word leapt down from heaven – reflected in the words of that popular carol , 'How silently, how silently, the wondrous gift is given ...'

And in many of his own works of healing, of bringing wholeness to those who come or who are brought to him Jesus performs his miracles away from the multitude ... aside from the crowd.

Again the gospel narratives are very clear that it is often when Christ himself is in the thick of it that he makes for the mountainside – he goes out onto the hillside, up into the mountains to pray, to stop, to look, to listen and, of course, it is the mightiest act of all, the raising of Jesus from the dead which is accomplished in the silence of the night, a night pierced with the radiance of God's glory, God's saving grace and love.

Paul urges us at Colossians 3:16, *Let the word of Christ dwell in you richly.* Well how can it be at all possible for that word of Christ so to dwell in us richly if we make no time or opportunity for it so to do – so that we can in stillness and silence ponder more deeply upon the sacred text and what God is saying to us through it. We certainly need to redress the imbalance between words and actions on the one hand and the lack of listening on the other – in the first place and quite crucially listening to God through his holy Word – listening to each other and not least those who from the same basis of the same God's holy Word may differ from us most sharply; listening, looking, being attentive to the world and its needs. Yet this quiet time classically understood and practised was not a quiet time of withdrawal into some privatised world of spiritual comfort – a pietism which is as Docetic as it is distorted – but rather this quiet time issuing in a passionate fervour for social justice and reform, the proclamation of God's kingdom of righteousness, justice, truth and peace. Many of the giants of social reform in the eighteenth and nineteenth centuries were evangelicals who having read, marked, learned and inwardly digested God's holy Word saw to it that that Word was not only a Word in season but a Word also in action. Where for example would Wilberforce and Shaftesbury have been without their Bibles? Wilberforce a member of the Clapham sect who worked indefatigably and with innumerable setbacks to ensure the passing of the Emancipation Act and the total abolition of slavery; and Shaftesbury and the Ten Hours Bill of 1847, the Factory Act of 1874 together with the Climbing Boys Act for young boys being pressed unlawfully into chimney cleaning.

And it wasn't only the names of the great, or for that matter, male persons either. As many if not more women were deeply involved in what might be described as the social agenda – social action.

One such, for example, was Hannah More, late-eighteenth/early-nineteenth century, deeply committed both to education and social reform. In her book with the very appropriate title *Practical Piety* she writes 'Genuine religion demands not merely an external profession of our allegiance to God, but an inward devotedness of ourselves to His service ... the happiness of a Christian does not consist in mere feelings which may deceive, nor in frames which can only be occasional; but in a settled, calm conviction that God and eternal things have the predominance in his heart'. She describes practical Christianity as the 'exercising ourselves unto Godliness'. And as one writer has said of her 'She was far in advance of many of her contemporaries in condemning any kind of religious intolerance because she considered it hindered growth in true piety – a piety rooted in prayer – at once direct, honest and passionate. For her prayer is the 'Lord, save us, we perish' of drowning Peter; the cry of faith to the ear of mercy'.

It must surely then be very clear that it is the holistic holding together both of prayer and action, of being and doing, of silence and of speaking which typifies true Christian vocation, discipleship and mission.

In his book *The Renewal of Anglicanism* Alistair McGrath points out the particular and distinctive contribution to Anglicanism both of the evangelical and the catholic movement. 'Evangelicalism', he writes, 'is without question the powerhouse of evangelistic endeavour within the modern church, in England and elsewhere'.

The catholic contribution he identifies as 'spirituality' – 'the long tradition of spiritual direction, which takes full account of the need for individual care and nurture in this respect'.

Having said that, quite rightly and properly he points out that 'a concern for spirituality need not be confined to the catholic wing of Anglicanism, any more than evangelism need be confined to its evangelical wing'. Amen to that! For it has been the whole thrust of my presentation this evening that it can never be either/or but must always be both/and – and to this end have attempted to demonstrate that there is indeed a rich tradition of spirituality, though that is not the way in which it may have been described – arising out of the evangelical movement. The quiet time, the time to stop, to look and to listen amidst the cacophonous clamours in both church and world is even more essential today than ever it has been. For if people out there – the world beyond the church – are only able to perceive 'church' in terms of 'politics, controversy, party spirit' – to use those words of Ryle – then what hope is there that the Gospel of Reconciliation with which we have been entrusted is likely even to be heard let alone taken seriously? And if the gospel – the good news of that abundance of life for all given us in Jesus Christ – becomes mired in our divisions and our fallings out, then we shall all stand condemned.

My hope and prayer for this conference is that in fanning the flame – the flame of the divine compassion, care and love bought so dearly on the cross for the salvation of the whole world – that flame may be kindled afresh and anew in each of us called to be bearers of good news, witnesses to the risen life of Christ, ourselves, our churches signs already here and now of God's kingdom come on earth as it is in heaven. But that cannot happen and it will not happen unless we make the time to stop, to look, to listen to God, 'the everlasting God, the creator of the ends of the earth' ... for only so will those who 'wait for the Lord renew their strength ... mount up with wings like eagles ... run and not be weary ... walk and not faint'.

Chapter 17

My Richest Gain I Count but Loss

Alister McGrath

Mark Noll, an American church historian, once made this point. He said, 'Our evangelicals write many good works of theology. But they are seen at their best in their hymns'. Why is this? It's because when we write hymns we are forced to ask: 'What is it about the Cross, about the gospel, that forces us to our knees, that makes us want to sing out in praise?'

This talk is bracketed by two great hymns. I am not going to be talking about evangelical hymnody, but I am going to be talking about what makes evangelicals want to write those great hymns of praise, about what has transformed their lives, about what has seized them, and given them this impetus to want to go on to convert, to challenge and to reach out to those in distress.

So I want simply to talk about the Cross, and our life as Christians. What is it about the Cross that made Isaac Watts say, 'My greatest gain I count but loss' in the light of this? The cross is the focus and the foundation of our faith. It brings us to our knees to raise us up; it draws us out of the world and then sends us back into that world to bring it this news of all that God has done for us and all that we know God will do for us in what lies ahead. And I speak to you as one who encountered that cross, was broken by it, and knows its power, because it forced me to confront my atheism, my deliberate rejection of God, and realise that there was something here that transcended anything I had ever known.

I was brought up in Northern Ireland as a kind of cradle Anglican. I was actually baptised by total immersion. This may seem ecumenical but it was accidental! What happened was that the Dean of the Cathedral who was baptising me had Parkinson's disease and to cut a long story short, he dropped me, and I was swallowed up by the waters of baptism and hastily retrieved! My colleagues at Wycliffe Hall say this explains a lot ... But I went on to reject Christianity – to say that it was not simply useless, but was actually evil. Then I encountered the proclamation of the gospel that changed the lives of those around me, those who bore in their lives the mark of the Cross of Christ, and I began to realise that I had got this one wrong. I needed to re-think, I needed to revisit, and in due course discovered the power of that gospel which I now proclaim to others. There are many who will complain that we don't respect each other's integrity in preaching like this. But I will say to you that I am an example of one whose integrity was challenged by the Cross, and I would date that point as being the moment at which I came to life. So the Cross changed me, it's changed you, and you and I know that it is this that is going to change us, to transform us, and to impel us out from this conference centre to bring this news to our nation.

The Cross speaks of many things, and today I only have time to speak of some. But to me one of the sadnesses is not so much that our nation has rejected the Cross. It's that it doesn't know enough about it to reject it in the first place. James Jones, whom you heard speak on Friday, tells a story of how he wanted to buy a cross for his daughter. He went into a jeweller's in the north of England and asked a young lady behind the counter whether she had any crosses. 'Yes', she said, 'Oh, we seem to have two sorts; there's this kind, then there's this other kind with a sort of little man on the cross ...' I think that is very significant, because for you and I that 'little man on the cross' is the basis of our life, our hopes and our mission. Yet she did not recognise it, really, as being anything. I think there is a real challenge to us here – to make sure that we go out and communicate this message of the Cross, so that people might realise that there is, indeed, something here that gives us a reason to hope and a reason to die; that there is something here which, even though we walk through the valley of the shadow of death, nothing can take away from us. So we need to confront our culture which simply does not know this, and we need also, I think, to remind ourselves that we probably know this story so well that it has lost its freshness. Maybe we need to revisit this and rediscover the Cross as if for the very first time.

My text this morning will be from 1 Corinthians chapters one and two, which speak of the Cross as a challenge to the wisdom, to the strength of the world. Paul says in 1 Corinthians 1:26:

Remember what you were, my brothers and sisters, when God called you. From the human point of view few of you were wise or powerful or of high social standing. But God deliberately chose what the world considers madness in order to shame the wise, and he chose what the world considers weak in order to shame the powerful. This means that no-one can boast in God's presence.

And there we have, I think, a challenge to rediscover a story that we know so well, and see it as if for the very first time.

I am sure you know the story of the professor and his chauffeur. This professor used to give a lecture; it was the same lecture, and he gave it time and time again. His driver got bored stiff. 'Can't you give a different story', he said. 'I know that one word for word; I have sat through it ten times. I know it word for word.' The professor said, 'Right. I will take you at your word. Next time we are changing places'.

So the next time duly came. The driver went to the front and sure enough, he knew it word for word. He gave the same lecture to the audience; they never knew the difference. But there was, actually, one difference. He spoke rather more quickly than the professor. At the end of the lecture the chairman looked at his watch and said, 'Oh, it seems that we have time for some questions. First question please'. And the first question was a killer. The lecturer who, remember, was the driver, looked the questioner straight in the eye, and said, 'That is such a stupid, simple question – I am going to ask my driver to answer it'.

We know the story of the crucifixion so well. What we need to remember is that, in our congregations, in our conversations, we will be talking to people who will not have heard it before; who will hear it from us for the very first time. The challenge to us is to convey its freshness, its life-changing capacity, and really to let that come to life, to refresh our vision of the Cross, to pray that God would outpour his Spirit upon us that our message truly would come to life and we present the Cross in all its radiance and all its wonder, that it might truly transform those we preach it to.

I am going to speak about two themes from the Cross: its challenge to us and its encouragement to us. It challenges the world, certainly. But I want today to speak more about the challenge that it poses to us – as those who see themselves as people under the authority of the Cross.

Many of you will know that one of the greatest preachers of the last century was Charles Haddon Spurgeon. A great man, a great ministry. His sermons would be preached on Sunday morning; by that same Sunday evening you could buy them on the streets of London. One of Spurgeon's best sermons was a sermon on repentance. The story is told of Spurgeon going on vacation to the West Country. It was a Sunday. He went to the local Methodist chapel and heard a local Methodist lay preacher preach a sermon. It was rather a good sermon, and it moved Spurgeon to tears. It was a sermon on repentance. Afterwards, Spurgeon introduced himself. The preacher was hopelessly embarrassed.

'Mr Spurgeon, I have just preached your sermon to you.' And Spurgeon wiped away the tears from his eyes and said, 'I know, but I needed someone to preach that to me'. I think the difficulty is that, sometimes, as evangelicals, we preach the Cross to others, and just need to be reminded that it bears on us as well. And it does speak words of judgement, uncomfortable words, that we need to hear.

If I may, I will simply touch on two themes where I think it challenges us. My two themes will be power and priorities.

Power

You saw from that brief extract I read from 1 Corinthians chapter 1 that the Cross critiques power. It is saying that God chose to make himself known to the world through weakness. One of our concerns is that, as evangelicals, we have grown in strength, grown in power. With that, I think, comes some temptations, and we need to be alert to these and know what to do in their face. We are often described as being a minority, as being marginalized. The latest figures from Ministry Division, looking at the number of students in our theological colleges, show that for the very first time, more than 70 percent of ordinands in full-time training are evangelicals. A recent British government report suggested that the British weren't very good at mathematics. But I would say to you: 70 percent – that's quite a minority! I think if our forebears back in NEAC1 in 1967 had known that would have happened, they would have been amazed. But I want to make the point, as Paul reminds us, there is no place for boasting. If we have succeeded, we have succeeded by God's grace, not by our merits. We need to reiterate this theme – success, if we dare use that word, is consistently the result of faithfulness on our part. We are called to be faithful, and if we succeed it is because we are faithful, and power can be something that is seriously misused.

I want to direct your attention to what is happening in New Westminster, Canada, where we have a liberal bishop who has clearly lost the theological argument, who has power but not credibility, and now can only win the day by using canon law to enforce his will on his diocese. If there were ever to be a Bishop Spong medal for overwhelming liberal braveness in the face of overwhelming theological arguments, I think Bishop Michael Ingham is going to win it in spades! And here's what I want to say. The liberals I knew when I was younger would say, 'Well, we don't agree with you in many of your perspectives but we respect you for what you are saying'. What we are seeing in New Westminster is an intellectually bankrupt liberalism which has lost the argument and in its desperation forces itself on others. I want to say to you, and you need to say to those you talk to, this is the unacceptable face of liberalism. It exposes the harshness, the dogmatism, the sheer bullying that lies beneath the surface. We need to pray for our brothers and sisters in New Westminster, and we need to let it be known that this is a liberalism which has lost its way, lost its arguments and can only sustain itself by sheer political power. Part of our responsibility is to make sure that this doesn't happen here.

You heard that very moving interview with David Short of St John's Shaughnessy on Sunday night[1]. One of the points he made in closing was very telling, 'We brought this upon ourselves: we didn't get involved'. I want to say to you – we need to get involved. We need to make sure that when there is a vacancy-in-see commission, we are fully represented on it. There is a real need for us to make sure we are fully involved in this.

But for us, we don't talk about power. The language is that of faithfulness and obedience. And the Cross elicits from us not triumphalism – we betray ourselves if we do that – but rather repentance, faithfulness and obedience. We have travelled a long way, that is true. There is much to give thanks for. But there is a long way still to go, and we need to be nourished, and we need to be nourished and sustained by God's faithfulness at every point along that journey. And I thank God that this is something that we can do, and something that we can look forward to. So, then, the Cross is a critique of power.

Priorities

But the Cross also is about priorities. 'My richest gain I count but loss.' There is always a challenge to us here; a challenge to us to ask difficult questions like this: 'Where is our true source of confidence? What is it that we really get excited about?'

For Paul in Philippians 3 everything is loss compared to the wonder of knowing Christ. That is a challenge to me and, I am sure, to others of you as well. For it forces me to ask this question: 'Is this true for me as I know it should be?' Maybe there are times when I can say, 'Yes'. But I fear I must tell you there are times when I say 'No', when other things have crept in, have somehow displaced Christ from his place of priority.

Martin Luther in his Greater Catechism offers us, I think, a real way of beginning to assess ourselves at this particular point. He says these words, 'Where your heart is and where your security is, that has become your God'. Those words are, I think, cathartic. They challenge us to look inside us and ask where our confidence really lies. Is it in the size of our congregation? Is it in the esteem in which we are held? Is it in our family, in our bank balances; where is it? Luther is inviting us to examine ourselves in order that we may re-assert the place of the Cross at the centre of our lives as individuals and as a movement. That, I think, brings us home always to the focus and the foundation of our faith. If we take our focus away from this we will become distracted and lose that central resource which brings us our reason for being here and going into the world with something we know has the power to transform it.

We also need to see things from God's perspective and not from ours. In that first chapter of 1 Corinthians Paul talks about God choosing things that the world sees as being foolish and weak, and we need to re-evaluate everything, because we instinctively think that we can only exercise a good ministry, only live out our lives as Christians, if we are ordained, if we are ministering in that big church with a membership of a thousand, or running that big para-church ministry with huge influence.

Paul, I think, would remind us of a different way of looking at things. Scripture constantly presents us with a pattern of God choosing ordinary people and doing the most extraordinary things through them. It is not who you are or where you are that matters. It is what you let God do through you. I think we need to rediscover the doctrine of providence – the idea that God has placed us where he might want us to be, and that there are things there that we are able to do that need to be done, and maybe we are the only people who are able to do that.

If you think of the long chain of events and people that sepa-rate us from the Great Commission, when Christ commanded the disciples to go and make disciples of all nations, between them and us there is an unbroken chain of faithful witness, of one saying to another, 'Have you heard?' And that has been passed down from them to us like a great relay race, as a torch passed from one generation to another. The challenge to us is to do for the next generation what the previous generation did for us. And that means that, wherever God has placed us, we need to say 'God has put us here for a reason. There are things we need to do, there are things we **can** do', and trust that God in his graciousness is going to take us and use us, and do great things for us which will be passed on to future generations – trusting in a God who is able to use us, despite our weakness. Trusting in a God who is able to do things through us, even though we look around and see things that distress us, that puzzle us, that bewilder us. But these bring us back to the Cross, the focus, the foundation of all that we do.

Encouragement

This brings me to my final point, which is that the Cross is an encouragement. Let me read from 1 Corinthians chapter 2 in which Paul speaks about the encouragement that the Cross is to him, and I trust to you as well:

When I came to you, my brothers and sisters, to preach God's mystery, I did not use great words and learning, for while I was with you I made up my mind to forget everything except Jesus Christ and him crucified. So when I came to you I was weak and trembling with fear, and my teaching and message were not delivered with skilful words of human wisdom, but with proof of the power of the Spirit of God.

Now I find in those words an encouragement. There is an encouragement because we are reminded that the gospel does not rest on human wisdom. We live in a rapidly changing age when ideas come in, and then go out – when what our predecessors believed as certain truths are abandoned or inverted by those who succeed them. What Paul is saying is that this gospel that you and I have the privilege of knowing and the greater privilege of proclaiming is not a human invention, is not something that is going to go out of date now or the next year or the next century, but rather is grounded in God himself.

It is his truth, and the God who raised our Lord Jesus Christ from the dead is behind that gospel, and is behind us and with us as we seek to proclaim this to our nation. That seems to me to make a point of fundamental importance. The gospel is true and it is relevant, and it is guaranteed as such by God himself.

The story is told of a government department which was seeking to hire media consultants. They brought in the first one for interview. 'What do you get when you add two and two?' they asked him.

The answer came back: 'Four'.

It was not the right answer.

'Next!'

The next potential media consultant came in, and they asked him, 'What do you get when you add two and two?'

The interviewee leaned forward conspiratorially and said, 'Whatever you want it to be'.

'You're hired!'

I think that is the problem we face with our culture. There is always the temptation to say to it what it wants to hear.

This passage I have been reading from offers us a very different approach. It is saying quite simply that we have been entrusted with a gospel which is not ours. It is a gospel which is God's, and we have the privilege of being the earthen vessels containing this great treasure. It is not ours – we are not free to change it, we are not free to mess around with it. It is our task to proclaim it. The key virtue is faithfulness.

Let me make it clear, that does not just mean that we can just repeat what Calvin said in the sixteenth century, what Watts said in the eighteenth century, what Spurgeon said in the nineteenth century, because the task to every generation is to proclaim the gospel to that generation in terms that it can understand, breaking down those communication barriers. But the non-negotiable is clear – the gospel is something that we have been entrusted with as stewards, and it is in its own intrinsic power that we must trust. William Inge, who was dean of St Paul's Cathedral for many years, left us with this one-liner which I think is very relevant here: 'Whoever marries the spirit of the age today is widowed tomorrow'. Our liberal friends I think have a temptation to adjust the gospel to make it relevant to whatever the latest cultural trend is. Our position is that of being faithful to the gospel and, indeed, asking in what way can we best proclaim this to communicate with whoever our audience is, but always on the assumption we need to be faithful to this gospel that has been entrusted to us.

I find that exciting and encouraging, and as I close I will tell you why. First, it means that we may be weak, but the strength of God is able to speak through us. Indeed, more than that – once we acknowledge our weakness we are more likely to trust in God's strength than to rely on our own.

Secondly, because it brings home to us that our future as a movement inside this Church, in our local churches, as individuals, rests not in our wisdom nor our achievements, but rather in the faithfulness of the God to whom we in turn seek to be faithful.

I end by going to 1 Thessalonians chapter 5, where Paul lays upon the Thessalonian church many responsibilities – 'Do this, do this, do this ...' Perhaps they were overwhelmed. Perhaps we are overwhelmed as we think of all the tasks ahead of us which we know we must fulfil. But, where there is a command, there is always a promise, and in 1 Thessalonians chapter 5 verse 24 Paul gives us this, and I leave it with you: *He who has called you is faithful, and he will do it.*

My dear brothers and sisters, there are so many things that need to be done, there are so many challenges that need to be faced. But we are not on our own, because we can rely on the strength and the power and the wisdom of the God who raised Christ Jesus from the dead, who has called each and every one of us to be his and to serve him, and who impels us from this platform out into that world, but not on our own, but hand in hand with him.

He who has called you is faithful, and he will do it. To that God be praise and glory for ever. Amen.

Notes

1. Revd David Short, Rector of St John's church, Shaughnessy, in Canada, was interviewed over the phone on the Sunday evening of NEAC, explaining the battles for orthodoxy he was then facing in the Diocese of New Westminster.

Chapter 18

Presidential Address

1 Thessalonians 2:1–12

Wallace Benn

I want to focus on verse 2 of 1 Thessalonians 2:1–12, as we look through these marvellous verses: ... *with the help of our God we dared to tell you his gospel.* Let me just remind you of the situation. Paul had evidently been accused. Carson and Moo in their *Introduction to the New Testament* say 'Paul had evidently been accused of a number of shortcomings. He had tricked the converts with his flatteries and the like. He was interested in their money rather than their spiritual progress. He had no love for them. In rebutting such accusations Paul brings out for evangelists and pastors of all time important lessons about the kind of lives they should live.' Or listen to the words of John Stott: 'In these chapters, more perhaps than anywhere else in his letters, Paul discloses his mind, expresses his emotions and bares his soul. No-one who has engaged in any form of parochial ministry, ordained or lay, can fail to be touched and challenged by what Paul writes here.' Or listen to Tom Wright: 'A passage that ought to be written out in large letters and hanging on the wall in every Christian minister's house, or perhaps better engraved in letters of gold on his or her heart.'

So these words are very important. But when I thought about what to say today I kept coming back to this passage which has meant so much to me.

Let's think for a few moments together about Paul as a mission-ary under four headings.

1. Paul's Message

Paul tells us repeatedly that he is proclaiming the gospel of God. Look at 2:2, *But as you know with the help of our God we dared to tell you his gospel* (literally, 'God's gospel') *in spite of strong opposition*; and 2:8, *We loved you so much that we were delighted to share with you not only the gospel of God but our lives as well*; and 2:9, *Surely you remember, brothers, our toil and hardship; we worked night and day in order not to be a burden to anyone while we preached the gospel of God to you.*' And down in 2:13 Paul changes the phrase, but it is a phrase with great power, he describes the gos-pel as *that which they proclaimed as the Word of God.*

Do you get the point? What Paul is proclaiming is not his own ideas. It is not his own spin on the revelation of God in Christ. It is not even what Christ means to him. It is the gospel of God, it is that which has been revealed by God and Paul is an entrusted messenger of that message.

Let's think again, and I thought at one point that Alister McGrath in his magnificent talk in the last session was going to steal almost this entire point. And he put it rather better than I could. But let us just think a little bit about the implications of what this means. This gospel, this gospel of God, is not to be tampered with. It is not to be watered down, or adjusted in any day or generation to make it more acceptable to those who Christians think will find it more acceptable if it were watered it down. As it is God's gospel and as it is the power of God to salvation to those who believe it is not to be watered down or altered in any way. We are entrusted with God's revelation, the good news of God's love to us in his Son, our Saviour Jesus Christ. And in a pluralistic and relativistic age it is always a temptation, to be under pressure to adjust the message, to make it better, as a kind of sales pitch in the supermarket of ideas. Paul said, 'I'd have none of that, for what I am proclaiming is the gospel of God.' By all means find new ways to speak relevantly into the generation in which we live, find news way of communicating the gospel, but don't alter the message, for it is God's gospel.

Listen to Leon Morris commenting on Paul's comment, 'we speak as men approved by God to be entrusted with the gospel' (2:4). He writes:

> The Christian preacher is always tempted to accommodate his message to the desires of his hearers. People do not want a message that tells them that they are helpless sinners and that they must depend humbly on God's mercy for their salvation. They are more interested in the social implications of the gospel – these of course must not be soft peddled. But the preacher must always put his emphasis of those doctrines to which Scripture itself gives priority.[1]

Or listen again to John Stott in his commentary on these words:

> No secret of Christian ministry is more important than its fundamental God centeredness. The stewards of the gospel are primarily responsible neither to the church, not to its synods, or leaders, but to God himself. It is God's gospel and it is not to be tampered with[2].

Secondly, an old friend of mine John Allen, who some of you will know, is a very acute observer of the church scene, said in 1990, he thought the problem for the church in England was that it was suffering from a loss of nerve. I hope that that is less true after a decade of evangelism, than it was when he said it. But I think that it is true. And if we are to be the gospel people that God calls us to be then we need by God's grace to rekindle that sense of nerve in our hearts about the treasure that has transformed our lives and that God has entrusted to us to proclaim.

And then we need to ask ourselves what is this gospel that Paul is preaching here? Because often in our churches there is a good deal of talk about the gospel, but what do we mean by the gospel?

Well, let us see what Paul means by the gospel. Look back with me at 1:9 as he reminds those Christians who have become so in Thessalonica, he says *your reputation has spread far and wide, they tell how you turned to God from idols to serve the living and true God.* Our own world has lots of idols. I like this definition, the best definition I know about what an idols is: 'anybody or anything that takes God's place in our lives'. They turned away from idols, to come to know the joy of serving the living and true God. And Paul says in 1:10 not only is it about repentance and turning away from idolatry to come to know and to serve the living and true God, but to wait for his Son from heaven – the eschatological dimension. To wait for God's Son returning from heaven whom God raised from the dead, Jesus who rescues us from the coming wrath. I hope you understand that your biggest problem is not your sin, my biggest problem is not my sin. My biggest problem is the attitude of a righteous God to my sin. And you see the good news of the gospel is that God in his love by the death of his Son has provided a solution, that you and I on the day of judgement might be covered in his righteousness, that we might stand in Christ, that is what a Christian means, in Christ. That we might not fear that day. Look how Paul goes on to describe this gospel that he is preaching, look down at 2:12 ... *encouraging, comforting and urging you to live lives worthy of God, who calls you into his eternal kingdom.* God, the one who has given us life, the one who has created the universe, is the one who issues a personal call through the gospel into his kingdom the place of his reign and protection and care and love, the realm of forgiveness. And he is willing to share his very glory with us. What a magnificent gospel this is! And Paul describes in 3:2 as *the gospel of Christ.* It is wrapped up in him. It is all about him and a relationship with him. That is the message that Paul proclaimed and that is the message which you and I are called to proclaim too.

2. Paul's Motivation

For the appeal we made does not spring from error or impure motives, nor are we trying to trick you. On the contrary we speak as men approved by God to be entrusted with the gospel. (1 Thessalonians 2:3–4)

You remember the situation described in Acts 16, Paul had been to Philippi. He had been in the words of the TNIV translation, *outrageously treated*. He had suffered and been insulted in Philippi. Actually Acts 16 tells us, and Luke records for us, that he was severely flogged. And the Romans knew how to beat someone to within an inch of their life. Paul was beaten like that in Philippi; he was arrested without trial and imprisoned. And do you remember there were a number of amazing conversions? But Paul had been horrendously treated in Philippi and now he recalls the next stop of his missionary journey, which was in Thessalonica.

I want you to imagine with me, what it might like to feel like to be on that kind of apostolic mission. Just imagine for a moment, that you had gone to preach the gospel down in Southport down the road. You had caused a riot, you had been beaten up and flogged and now you are here in Blackpool. Wouldn't the temptation be to have an apostolic sabbatical? To say: 'God understands, it is time I put my feet up. I need to tone down things a bit, because it has got a little bit too hot.' No, Paul says, in spite of all that, with the help of our God, we dared to tell you his gospel.

3. Paul's Manner of Life

And then think of Paul's manner of life. Paul put himself out in the service of this gospel. You see he didn't just preach a message, he actually lived it out. Look at what he said in 2:8: *we loved you so much that we were delighted to share with you not only the gospel of God but our lives as well, because you had become so dear to us. Surely you remember, brothers, our toil and hardship; we worked night and day in order not to be a burden to anyone while we preached the gospel of God to you.*

Paul put himself out, he gave of himself in love to the people he wanted to serve and communicate the good news of the gospel to. And I think of a story that the man who led me to Christ, Dai Lewis, a Scripture Union evangelist, used to tell, about a next-door neighbour of his, that he and his wife prayed for often and for a long time. They never got an opportunity to share the gospel, no matter how hard they tried to get alongside their neighbour it didn't seem to work. And then one day he realised that his neighbour was really obsessed with sailing. So Dai, who had never sailed a dinghy in his life and was prone to seasickness, went down to the library and bought all the books that he could on sailing and read them up. And then leant over the garden wall and said, 'I see you've got a dinghy there, that's very interesting ... I've been reading this and that'. And the neighbour said to him 'Gosh I didn't know you were into sailing'. And Dai said, 'Yes, well, you know I've been reading up about it'. Well, the neighbour said, 'Will you come with me next weekend? I've been looking for a crew member'.

Dai said he never prayed so much in that week as in any other time. Do you know what happened? They went sailing that week-end. The neighbour decided that his Christian neighbour was an OK chap. And he invited him back the following weekend and on the following weekend he gave his life to Christ. You see Dai had put himself out in the service of the gospel. Paul here says he acted as a mother (2:7) ... *we were gentle among you, like a mother caring for her little children* and like a father in 2:11 in instruction ... *we dealt with you as a father deals with his own children, encouraging, comforting and urging you to live lives worthy of God.*

My dear friends, brothers and sisters, can I ask us all: 'Will evangelical ordinands go to the hard places?' For I find some who want to go to Holy Trinity Brompton or St Helen's or All Souls, depending on the shade.

Will we go to the hard places and the tough places? Will we live in the house that doesn't quite have the kitchen that we'd like it to have? Will we put ourselves out in the service of the gospel? Will we as gospel people go to the edge with the kind of Pauline commitment we see here? For that is what Paul did.

4. Paul's Means

Paul says *we had boldness in our God, we dared to tell you the gospel*. We need God to help us don't we, for our get-up-and-go not to have got-up-and-went. We need to get that more daring: loving daring, caring daring, sensitive daring, in gospel ministry.

Let me remind you of a statistic that again just reinforced the kind of things we all know and that we have been hearing about this congress. Over 50 percent of people surveyed recently could not name the four Gospels.

I hope you are coming from a growing church, I know that in all the groupings in the church we are growing the most, but listen, overall against the huge secular tide in our nation we are not winning. Don't we need to have a new daring in the cause of the gospel? We are called to be conservative in theology, faithful to the revelation of God in Christ, and to the apostolic witness to that, there in the pages of the New Testament for us. But we are called to be radical in zeal to get the gospel across, in love to build bridges to the people amongst whom we live and who we seek to serve, in order that we may be able to share Christ in a meaningful way. How radical are we prepared to be? Don't we need to be much more focussed in terms of evangelism and mission?

When I was in Harold Wood as a Vicar, I remember we thought ourselves, I guess at that time, to be at that time a kind of flagship evangelical church, and we were shocked to discover that there was a whole age grouping and culture grouping of people in our parish who we had never touched with the gospel and I'd love to tell you the story of how we got a community centre which was on sale for a million pounds, we got it for a pound a year for twenty years and began a youth work, because God opened the door. And we were reminded again that just a little step of faith from us, God is there and opens the door.

One of the most exciting things I have been involved with as a Bishop has been in doing a series of events called 'Party on the Pier' along the south coast. And we took night clubs and we invited a lot of young people to come, more than half of whom were un-churched, and I became convinced again that if we communicate the gospel in a way that is relevant and can be heard culturally by the people we are seeking to communicate it to – they will respond, because they did in droves and it was thrilling to hear it. Don't we need to get back the kind of heart we heard from Andy Hawthorne,[3] and saw in him, a heart for the lost, a heart to get the gospel out?

Brothers and sisters, we have a large mission task to engage with, but doesn't Paul help us here to do that, to have the right kind of conviction and motivation? You know over the years we have asked ourselves the question, 'What does it mean to be an evangelical?' I know of no better answer than the answer of this passage, and by the way isn't it good to be an evangelical in this sense, in this sense, isn't it good to be an evangelical? Let us have a joy about that, let us have a confidence about the message that God has given to us, and let us have a new daring to get it out.

The Archbishop of Canterbury wrote recently that the months and years ahead in our church and in the Anglican communion are likely to be messy. We need a deep and evangelical unity to stand together with this kind of gospel heart. And not only an evangelical unity, but we need a love and a willingness to reach out our hands and join hands with co-belligerents as we face some of the challenges in the church, with co-belligerents who are credally and morally orthodox. That is why I am thrilled about *Anglican Mainstream*, which I personally hope you will be able to support.

But above all we need courage. We need faithfulness to God's gospel and to God's Word. But in any controversial situation we may find ourselves in, of having stand for things which swim against the tide of the views of our day and generation. In any controversy we need to keep the gospel heart that we see here in the apostle Paul. We need to keep his priorities at the top of our priorities.

Sisters and brothers, we need a renewed faithfulness to God, to his gospel and his Word. And a new daring in God to carry the good news to a world that desperately, desperately needs to hear it. May these things that marked out the Apostle Paul, may they mark us out to the glory of Jesus. Amen.

Notes

1. Leon Morris, *1 and 2 Thessalonians* (Leicester: Inter Varsity Press, 1956) p.45
2. *Op. cit.* p.50
3. In an earlier Congress talk.

Letter from the Steering Committee to Anglicans in North America

During the Congress we heard from the Very Revd Dr Peter Moore, from Trinity Episcopal School in Ambridge, Pennsylvania, about problems affecting ECUSA, and Revd David Short from St John's Church, Shaughnessy, Vancouver, joined in by phone about the troubles that Canadian Anglicans are facing. Paul Gardner read out a letter of support from the Steering Committee.

To Our Sisters and Brothers on the North American Continent

Dear Brothers and Sisters

We write to you as members of the Steering Committee of the Fourth National Evangelical Anglican Congress now taking place in Blackpool, England. We rejoice together in our fellowship in Christ.

We know of the attacks that you have had to withstand in recent months and years. These attacks on so many areas of our shared biblical faith have been severe and stressful for many of you and we weep with you.

We write to assure you of our deepest prayers and support.

We pray also that he who is our Lord and Saviour will encourage you all to stand firm.

We are also praying for our Archbishop of Canterbury, Dr Williams, and for the Primates meeting in October. We pray that God will bring great wisdom to their deliberations and that they will affirm and uphold the orthodox and biblical faith that we have received through God's providence across the ages.

May God give you grace to stand firm and persevere in this time of trial.

Yours in the grace and peace of Christ.

Paul D. Gardner
Chairman of NEAC4
On behalf of the steering committee
22 September, 2003

The Way
Forward

Chairman's Reflections after the Congress

Paul Gardner, Chairman, Church of England Evangelical Council

The gathering of just over two thousand Anglican evangelical leaders at Blackpool in September 2003 was undoubtedly an exceptional occasion. More than fifteen years had passed since the previous gathering in Caister. Throughout the three years during which it was being drawn together, the many divisions among the different types and styles of evangelicals often threatened to defeat the planners. Nevertheless, when it finally happened, most people felt it was a wonderful time of restoring friendships and relationships and of learning together. Under the uniting theme of 'Bible, Cross and Mission' many speakers, representing a good variety of positions, demonstrated just how much there was that united evangelicals while, at the same time, highlighting areas that needed further examination among ourselves.

There was a deliberate policy of exposing as many speakers to the evangelical constituency as possible, thus breaking away from only inviting the 'gurus' of our tradition. This was exciting for us all as we began to realise, even just by looking at the speaker list, how God had blessed us with many men and women from whom we could all learn a great deal. In all, over 150 people spoke in various sessions, whether in smaller group or to the whole gathering. Since then, we have seen just how often some of those speakers have been called upon to offer help around the country and to speak again to their areas of expertise. Of course, in seeking to use so many contributors a number of issues arose. Main stage speakers were largely limited to between 20 and 25 minutes each which meant, for some, that it was quite difficult to develop the depth of argument they would have liked. It was also notable that there was often not enough time for questions or space for continuing discussion, but that was a choice that had to be made as the planners sought to bring on board people who would represent different types of evangelicals with different experiences.

Reflecting back on the Congress from the vantage point of a year on, there are some serious problems I believe we must continue to address and some exciting possibilities that are already being driven forward.

First among the serious problems needing to be faced is the apparent inability of some evangelicals even to want to listen to others with whom they may disagree. This reflected itself in a variety of ways before the Congress. There were those who immediately went to the Press whenever they felt they might have heard something they didn't quite 'like' from the planning committee. Usually the rumours were quite false. Often the facts had not even been checked and it seemed as though the biblical approach of talking through differences with each other simply didn't 'figure on their agenda'. Mixed up with this were those who were upset that they had not been invited to speak. Certainly we encountered a degree of arrogance among some that at times left us gasping. Then there were those who would not come because they felt the speakers were too 'liberal' or too 'conservative', and those who eventually came only to criticise the event. There is no doubt that as the Church of England Evangelical Council takes things forward, high on their agenda must be the need to enable us all to talk together and to behave in a more Christian and, dare I say, mature manner. But CEEC will not be able to manage this on its own. The Diocesan Evangelical Fellowships and Unions are well placed to take the initiative here. Talking together and doing mission together at more local levels will also be one valuable way of enabling us all to see how much evangelicals have in common. There are many groupings among evangelicals and some of these rarely attend their local Diocesan Evangelical Fellowships. A much greater effort will be needed here on all sides. CEEC needs also to be a catalyst to encourage those groupings themselves to reach out to others and to engage in conversation and serious theological discussion.

Secondly, I believe there is often a fear of theological debate. So many evangelicals now live in a largely pragmatic way that debate and discussion are seen either to be of no special use or else to be 'unloving' or 'unspiritual'. The planners also encountered much of this. If this is not serious for this generation, and I believe it is, it will certainly be dangerous for the next generation if serious theological discussion around Scripture is not taking place among us. 'If it works, it must be OK' is a recipe for disaster a few years down the line. It is high time that we developed ways of challenging each other theologically without either implying we are superior to the other or feeling threatened by the other.

This really will call for a greater degree of Christian love for and commitment to each other, and a much stronger attempt to phrase challenges and debates in such a way that we communicate that love and concern without alienating each other. Perhaps we shall have to work harder at finding the things we agree upon before always heading straight for the areas where we disagree with each other. This we hope is what was modelled at NEAC. Of course, it led to criticism that we did not really engage at a deep level with differences among us, but we certainly did begin to develop a greater degree of trust together, and so open the way forward for those who wish to pursue a deeper degree of interaction in future.

However, it is the exciting possibilities ahead of us which should preoccupy us. As NEAC has been and is being followed up in a whole variety of ways, we are seeing more and more clearly how our commitment to the Christ who bore our sins on the cross by dying in our place, and who rose from the dead and now reigns in glory, is a uniting message that we can together take into our country without compromise. We have seen more clearly than in a generation how the fervour for evangelism and outreach had not waned over the years, and we see some of the most exciting initiatives in evangelism and church planting are being brought forward by evangelicals. Here is clear evidence of the Holy Spirit at work among us, and we must live and work with grateful thanks to God for his grace among us.

In the Providence of God, the Congress occurred at an extraordinary time in the history of the Church of England. An attempt had just been made to consecrate a bishop in Reading who had been in a practising homosexual relationship and who, though now celibate, had never repented of this former relationship. Indeed, his teaching was and remains clearly committed to seeking a change in the church's attitude to 'faithful homosexual relationships'. In the end, traditional Anglican teaching won through and the person concerned withdrew from the appointment (though he has recently now been made a Dean of a cathedral). The problem for most evangelicals, and for those of us organising NEAC, was that this move simply confirmed how far the 'liberal tradition' was making inroads into changing the culture and theology of our Church. Above all, it demonstrated so clearly how far so many church leaders had moved from treating biblical teaching as the standard by which we should always be judging ourselves, our actions and our thinking. At the Congress a message of support was sent from the organisers to Canadian clergy of the New Westminster Province who were being heavily attacked for standing against their Bishop. That Bishop and the synod were moving towards the acceptance of 'blessings' for homosexual relationships.

Against this background, then, the reaffirmation of the God-breathed nature of all Scripture was all the more remarkable and necessary. What shone through in this Congress was just how committed evangelical Anglicans remain to affirming that God speaks to his people of today through his Word in Scripture. While many of us would have liked more time and more discussion around vital hermeneutical issues, this could come later. In a context of a national church that seemed so widely to be rejecting any traditional understanding of the nature, role or teaching of Scripture, the necessity for us all as evangelicals lay in re-affirming our commitment to that Word. Certainly we are living in a time when God's Word written in

Scripture is being attacked from within the church more openly and more savagely than ever before.

Throughout the Congress we were also reminded that we are part of an international communion. Again and again we recognised how much we had to learn, or re-learn, from Anglican brothers and sisters in the countries of the Global South. Their dynamism, their fervent preaching of the gospel, their commitment to following the Christ of Scripture and his Word, their preparedness to suffer even to the point of death, all helped contextualise our own preoccupations more clearly within God's purposes for his whole world. We were reminded too of the inherent racism so often coming through from liberal western theologians who attack as 'naive' or 'primitive' the desire of so many Africans, Asians and South Americans to obey the God who speaks in Scripture.

There is much that we all yet have to face. Even as I write we await the outcome of the 'Lambeth (Eames) Commission' looking at divisions within the Anglican communion. Evangelicals will find themselves constantly having to defend and fight for biblical orthodoxy. We will find partners in other sections of the Anglican communion, and we will need to ensure we do not let down our guard. We must be alert at local level, at Diocesan level, and at national church level. And we must always be seeking to work together on such vital issues as we highlighted at this Congress – Bible, Cross and Mission. Let us pray together that we may indeed. *Guard the good deposit that was entrusted to [us] – guard it with the help of the Holy Spirit who lives in us* (2 Timothy 1:14). And let us never take lightly Peter's warning, *Therefore, dear friends, since you already know this, be on your guard so that you may not be carried away by the error of lawless men and fall from your secure position* (2 Peter 3:17).

We want to hear from you. Please send your comments about this book to us in care of zreview@zondervan.com. Thank you.

GRAND RAPIDS, MICHIGAN 49530 USA

ZONDERVAN.COM/
AUTHOR**TRACKER**